Love First

We Can Love because God Loved Us First!

By
Kent Mankins, Ph.D., M.Ed.

Contents

Introduction

"Which commandment is the most important of all?" Jesus answered, "The most important is, 'Hear, O Israel: The Lord our God, the Lord is one. And you shall love the Lord your God with all your heart and with all your soul and with all your mind and with all your strength.' The second is this: 'You shall love your neighbor as yourself.' There is no other commandment greater than these."
Mark 12:28-31

The concept of *love first* was born as a result of pressure from our pastoral staff at Valley Assembly. While the church had a mission statement, "Passionate Pursuit of God and Compulsive Compassion for People," our team did not feel it adequately represented who we were and what God had called us to do. Since I was the one who had formed that statement, I was somewhat (okay, extremely) resistant to changing it. I was also, if truth be told, a little (okay, highly) offended they didn't appreciate our mission statement. After all, it had alliteration and I love alliteration!

After a long and robust discussion, I finally acquiesced and agreed to consider a new statement. I began tossing ideas out to the team which they repeatedly rejected. They pushed and pushed for more.

Out of frustration, I sat and prayed silently. When I let go of my ideas and my agenda, the Holy Spirit spoke: "Love first. We can love because He first loved us." Every person around the table declared, "This is our calling."

Love first is a calling, not only for our church but for all followers of Jesus. When we love first, we place God and others before ourselves. When we love first, we fulfill Jesus' greatest commandments!

Part 1
Love First:
God Loved First

Chapter 1
God Loves First!

We love because he first loved us.

1 John 4:19

My heart sank as I listened to a prominent preacher proclaim that when a person commits a particular type of sin, he or she is disqualified from being used by God. I hurt for the many people I personally know who have stumbled in this area, and my heart hurt for me. This external voice was, once again, a reminder that I am not good enough. Usually that voice comes from inside or perhaps from the enemy who is constantly trying to defeat me with accusations that God cannot possibly love me, much less work through me. I have wrestled with these feelings of not being good enough for most of my life.

How about you? How much confidence do you have that you are good enough for God? If you have not yet entered a relationship with Jesus, not considering yourself as good enough may be part of the reason you haven't accepted His invitation. If you are a Christ-follower, not being good enough may be a challenge with which you constantly wrestle. If you are like me, every time you stumble is a palpable reminder of your insufficiency.

Regardless of where you are in your journey with Jesus, you have probably wrestled with this idea of personal shortcoming, or I am sure you at least know someone who has.

This isn't a new struggle or even a new accusation from those who consider themselves religious leaders. In fact, Jesus encountered a woman who was told by religious leaders that she wasn't good enough. But I am sure she didn't need someone else to tell her that. She lived a lifestyle I am confident was accompanied by the constant inner nagging that she would never be good enough. Yet these leaders didn't feel her internal war was enough condemnation. They publicly shamed her, declaring she was so unforgivable, she deserved brutal death by stoning.

And yet, Jesus graciously forgave her! As she stumbled away, the dust still thick in the air, she asked herself, "What just happened?" The last few minutes had been a whirlwind of terrifying emotion as she faced, most surely, were what to be her final few minutes alive. The Law was clear, and she knew it. She was caught in the act. Her guilt was unquestionable. Her sentence was death. As she turned and looked back at the scene of her would-be execution, only one individual remained. Her accusers had left, one by one, leaving only the man responsible for her freedom . . . for her life. Their eyes met, and without saying a word, she began to weep.

She contemplated this stranger's words, "I do not condemn you ... go and sin no more."

"Who is this man? Who gave him the right to pronounce my freedom?" She didn't know the answers to her questions, but one thing was certain. She owed this man her life. Her heart flooded with gratitude and love.

The story of this nameless woman in the Gospel of John, chapter 8, is one of the most loved in the entire Bible. The woman really was an extra in this scene. The religious leaders who brought her to Jesus were not concerned as much with her sin as they were with catching Jesus in a trap. Really, any lawbreaker would have done.

However, as God so often does, He turned their treachery into an opportunity to demonstrate His character. Jesus knew the letter of the Law required death for the act of adultery, and He also knew the hearts of the men who brought her before Him. They all had sinned and therefore had no right to cast the first stone. Her accusers left, John recorded, beginning with the oldest and, obviously, the wisest.

Why is this brief story so loved? Because I am that woman . . . you are that woman. We have all been caught in the act of sin and we are all undoubtedly guilty. We also know the penalty for our sin is the same that the woman faced: death.

The Apostle Paul wrote, "For the wages of sin is death, but the gift of God is eternal life in Christ Jesus our Lord" (Romans 6:23). To see the grace the Son of God so compassionately poured out on this sinful woman gives us a glimpse of how He deals with us, and that moves us deeply.

Some believe this nameless woman the Apostle John wrote about is the same one who, in the Gospel of Luke, approached Jesus as He, His followers, and Simon reclined at the table. She broke open an alabaster jar of expensive perfume, poured the perfume on Jesus' feet, and wiped His feet with her hair. The Bible is unclear about who she was; however, it is crystal clear that Jesus responded to the woman written of in the Gospel of Luke with equal compassion, mercy, and grace as He did to the woman described in the Gospel of John.

The actions of the woman in the Gospel of Luke raised more than a few eyebrows. Here was a woman wiping this great teacher's feet with expensive perfume and her own hair . . . that's questionable enough. But she was also a woman who lived a sinful life! When questioned about the appropriateness of the woman's actions, Jesus told a story:

> *"A certain moneylender had two debtors. One owed five hundred denarii, and the other fifty. When they could not pay, he cancelled the debt*

of both. Now which of them will love him more?"

Simon answered, "The one, I suppose, for whom he cancelled the larger debt."

And he said to him, "You have judged rightly." Then turning toward the woman, he said to Simon, "Do you see this woman? I entered your house; you gave me no water for my feet, but she has wet my feet with her tears and wiped them with her hair. You gave me no kiss, but from the time I came in she has not ceased to kiss my feet. You did not anoint my head with oil, but she has anointed my feet with ointment. Therefore, I tell you, her sins, which are many, are forgiven—for she loved much. But he who is forgiven little, loves little." (Luke 7:41-47)

Why did this woman love Jesus so much? Because whoever has been forgiven little loves little, but she had been forgiven much. She recognized she was sinful and deserved a severe sentence, and Jesus was merciful . . . *Jesus loved first!*

In both stories, we see a beautiful picture of God's undeserved and unearned love. But it is not only in these outrageous acts of Jesus' grace and mercy that we see God's love. We see His love from the very beginning. In the very act of creation, we find God loved first!

God Has Loved First Since the Beginning!

In the beginning, there was nothing. Have you ever considered *why* God created the world? Perhaps He simply decided one day to get creative. Perhaps He simply got bored. Or perhaps He desired to create someone with whom He could have intimate relationship. I have often wondered why God would choose to create humankind, knowing the pain we would cause Him and each other.

Being all-knowing, God surely knew we would not make it far into our existence without failing Him. Surely, He knew from the beginning the price that would have to be paid for our redemption. Yet He still chose to create us. He still chose the path leading to heartache and pain. Why?

I am not sure there is an absolutely certain answer to that question. The Bible doesn't explicitly address it. However, I think it is possible to look at the story of God's pursuit of humankind over the millennia and arrive at some plausible conclusions.

> If God *is love*, God has always *been* love, and love needs an object!

The Apostle John writes that God is love (1 John 4:8). If God *is love*, God has always been love, and love needs an object! Love is not simply a feeling but an action. God's creation of the world and of humankind is our first insight into God's character, into God's love. God took special effort to create the perfect habitat for humankind to inhabit. Creation was *all good!* Then He created man. But God looked at man and said that it is not good for man to be alone (Genesis 2:18).

This is the first time in all of creation God did not reflect that what He created was wholly good. God could have said, "I will be enough for this man." Instead, He created a woman to be a partner for the man. Then, "God saw everything that he had made, and behold, it was very good. And there was evening and there was morning, the sixth day" (Genesis 1:31).

With the final act of creating the woman for the man, God deemed that His creation was not only good but *very good.* In the act of creating woman for man, God demonstrated love by caring for man's well-being. God not only cared for man by providing a perfect habitat and a partner, and He then gave the man and woman ownership of everything He had created!

> God's love was demonstrated from the beginning in His care for humanity's physical, social, emotional, and spiritual needs.

God's love was demonstrated from the beginning in His care for humanity's physical, social, emotional, and spiritual needs. Regardless of the pain He knew we would cause Him and each other, He must have been able to look past the pain to the joy of intimately knowing, caring for, and interacting with those who would choose to accept His love and return their love to Him.

The King James Version interpretation of Revelation 4:11 says, "Thou art worthy, O Lord, to receive glory and honour and power: for thou hast created all things, and for thy pleasure they are and were created." Here we find insight into why God created this world. He created this world, you included, for His pleasure. His creation brings Him pleasure! You and I were created for God's pleasure. He loved us first, and because of that, we love Him.

I have had the privilege of traveling to many beautiful places in this world. I love the mountains, and my wife loves the ocean. We are a great example of surf and turf. Everywhere I go, from deserts to rain forests, from mountains to oceans, I marvel at the majestic creativity of our God. I then remember that before Adam and Eve disobeyed God, the world was even more awe-inspiring than now. Regardless of how breathtaking our beautiful world is now, what we see is the broken product of sin.

> *For the creation waits with eager longing*
> *for the revealing of the sons of God. For the*
> *creation was subjected to futility, not willingly,*
> *but because of him who subjected it, in*
> *hope that the creation itself will be set free from*
> *its bondage to corruption and obtain the*
> *freedom of the glory of the children of God.*
> (Romans 8:19-21)

God's intent from the beginning was that humankind would inhabit and rule over the perfect world He had created. But Adam and Eve didn't make it very far into the story before stumbling and destroying perfection.

After being tempted by Satan and eating the fruit of the forbidden tree, they became aware of their nakedness. It was this act of disobedience that transformed the course of history. God's perfect creation was now broken, and I believe God grieved as He saw the pain we would inflict on His creation, ourselves, each other, and ultimately, on His one and only son. However, none of this could have come as a surprise to the Almighty.

God wasted no time in confronting Adam and Eve, yet His confrontation was visibly grounded and perpetrated in love. Rather than a confrontation to demean and humiliate an already embarrassed Adam and Eve, God asked questions.

And they heard the sound of the Lord God walking in the garden in the cool of the day, and the man and his wife hid themselves from the presence of the Lord God among the trees of the garden. But the Lord God called to the man and said to him, "Where are you?"

And he said, "I heard the sound of you in the garden, and I was afraid, because I was naked, and I hid myself."

He said, "Who told you that you were naked? Have you eaten of the tree of which I commanded you not to eat?" (Genesis 3:8-11)

God's gentle questioning leads Adam and Eve to their own confession of their disobedience.

The consequences of their disobedience were severe for them, creation, and for us. God could have wiped the slate clean and started over then and there, but He didn't. Instead, He met them where they were and provided a covering for their sin.

The physical covering of fig leaves they had made was insufficient, so God sacrificed an animal to provide skins as the covering for their physical nakedness. Here we have the first picture of God's mercy and grace demonstrated in a physical act with spiritual implications. This animal sacrifice was representative of the sacrificial system God would provide for His people to experience the temporary forgiveness of their sin—a system that foreshadowed the ultimate sacrifice He would eventually supply in His son's death on the cross.

God Loved First when He Sent His Son!

As the story of God's pursuit of humankind continues, we find people repeatedly disobeying Him. Throughout the Scriptures, the people of Israel and God have a yo-yo relationship. God gives commands, the people disobey, God disciplines (or threatens to discipline), the people repent and offer sacrifices, and God forgives and blesses. This routine is repeated multiple times. As I read through Old Testament stories, I am always amazed and confounded by the amount of grace and mercy God had on His people. And I am grateful. I am grateful because I know the same depth of grace and mercy He poured out on them, He offers to me as well. He loves first, and we rarely deserve it!

> He loves first, and we rarely deserve it!

As history progressed, God sent prophets to tell of the day when a savior would come and be the final sacrifice for the sin of the people. The continual offering of the blood of animals would become obsolete when the final and perfect sacrifice was offered. The Apostle Paul wrote:

But when the fullness of time had come, God sent forth his Son, born of woman, born under the law, to redeem those who were under the law, so that we might receive adoption as sons. (Galatians 4:4-5)

At just the right moment in history, God sent Jesus. Again, and in a profound act of loving first, God took the initiative. He sent His one and only son to come and lay down His life as a sacrifice.

Through Jesus' sacrifice and our faith in Him, we are adopted into God's family as His own sons and daughters.

See what kind of love the Father has given to us, that we should be called children of God; and so we are. The reason why the world does not know us is that it did not know him. (1 John 3:1)

We didn't deserve this sacrifice, and we can't earn it . . . Christ's life was a demonstration of God's lavish love!

The first chapter of the Gospel of John tells us that Jesus came to His own people, but they did not receive Him. From the beginning of Jesus' life on earth, He was rejected and despised. King Herod, threatened by the news of Jesus' birth, gave orders to have every boy less than two years of age killed. Jesus' life was riddled with controversy and ridicule. Religious leaders called Him a blasphemer and constantly tried to trip Him up to disprove His message. As Jesus' popularity as a teacher grew, so did the animosity.

Why did Jesus come to give His life for a people He knew would be so resistant to receiving His teachings and sacrifice? Because He loved first! Many of us have memorized John 3:16, but it is important to read that passage in context.

> *For God so loved the world, that he gave his only Son, that whoever believes in him should not perish but have eternal life. For God did not send his Son into the world to condemn the world, but in order that the world might be saved through him. Whoever believes in him is not condemned, but whoever does not believe is condemned already, because he has not believed in the name of the only Son of God. And this is the judgment: the light has come into the world, and people loved the darkness rather than the light because their works were evil.* (John 3:16-19)

"For God so loved." That is the foundation of why Jesus came. Because Jesus loved first, He came to give His life to save those who would believe. He knew many would reject or despise Him, but He also knew there would be some who would choose to follow Him. There would be those who would see the light, love the light, and live in the light! Jesus knew some would receive Him. In John 1:12, John wrote that to all who believed Jesus and accepted Him, God gave the right to become His children.

> From the beginning, we see our God loving first in creation, in sacrifice, in mercy and grace, and ultimately in sending His only son, Jesus.

From the beginning, we see our God loving first in creation, in sacrifice, in mercy and grace, and ultimately in sending His only son, Jesus. The Apostle Paul wrote to the Romans that all have sinned, and the wages of sin is death. When we, like the woman caught in adultery and the sinful woman with her jar of oil, recognize that we have sinned and deserve the death penalty, we will be overwhelmed with gratitude. We have been forgiven by an outrageous act of love, demonstrated by Jesus' sacrifice on the cross, poured out when we did not deserve it. And that outrageous love inspires our love in return!

God shows his love for us in that while we were still sinners, Christ died for us. (Romans 5:8)

God took the initiative.

God took the first step.

God loved first!

Reflect . . .

1. In what ways did Jesus demonstrate love to the woman caught in adultery?

2. How did she respond to Jesus' love?

3. In what ways did God love you first?

4. How does His initiative in loving you equip you to love Him?

5. How does His initiative in loving you equip you to love others?

Chapter 2
Jesus: Past, Present, and Future

Jesus Christ is the same yesterday, today, and forever.

Hebrews 13:8

Have you ever been in a really difficult situation and had someone come alongside you to help with something you couldn't do yourself? Maybe you were sick. Maybe you were moving. Maybe you were finishing your basement.

My wife's and my first home was a fixer-upper with an unfinished basement. It was a continual project. After almost two years, we completed remodeling the upstairs. We thought we would finish the basement after taking a break from our labor; however, soon we discovered my wife was pregnant with our first child.

We knew we needed to complete the basement to have room for our growing family. This job required more than painting and pulling up carpet. It required carpentry, electrical, and plumbing skills. I had exactly *none* of the prerequisites! We couldn't afford to hire those jobs out, so I asked friends to help.

We were very blessed with skilled and loving friends who happily *(I think)* volunteered to help us out. This was not a couple of hours on a Saturday job. For several months, our friends came by the house whenever they had free time. They spent many hours, expended their energy, and got into the trenches to help us do something we absolutely could not have done ourselves.

> When someone steps in and gets their hands dirty, works beside us, and goes out of their way to help, it demonstrates they genuinely care about us.

When someone steps in and gets their hands dirty, works beside us, and goes out of their way to help, it demonstrates they genuinely care about us.

Although many are unaware, every single human has experienced someone helping us by doing something we were unable to do on our own. We are all unable to pay the price for the forgiveness of our own sin. We have all sinned (Romans 3:23) and the wages of our sin is death (Romans 6:23). Our right standing with God cannot be gained by keeping all the rules and regulations of the Law. In Jesus, God did for us what we could not do ourselves.

Now the birth of Jesus Christ took place in this way. When his mother Mary had been betrothed to Joseph, before they came together she was found to be with child from the Holy Spirit. And her husband Joseph, being a just man and unwilling to put her to shame, resolved to divorce her quietly. But as he considered these things, behold, an angel of the Lord appeared to him in a dream, saying, "Joseph, son of David, do not fear to take Mary as your wife, for that which is conceived in her is from the Holy Spirit. She will bear a son, and you shall call his name Jesus, for he will save his people from their sins." All this took place to fulfill what the Lord had spoken by the prophet:

"Behold, the virgin shall conceive and bear a son, and they shall call his name Immanuel" (which means, God with us).

When Joseph woke from sleep, he did as the angel of the Lord commanded him: he took his wife, but knew her not until she had given birth to a son. And he called his name Jesus.
(Matthew 1:18-25)

Jesus, Immanuel, God with us. Yes, *God* with us. Jesus was born fully God and fully man. As God, He always has been, always is, and always will be God with us! Hebrews 13:8 tells us that Jesus is the same yesterday, today, and forever. And in Revelation (4:8), we find a similar proclamation, "Holy, holy, holy is the Lord God Almighty, who was, and is, and is to come."

Past: Jesus *Was* God with Us!

Years ago, when I was a young lead pastor, one of the prominent leaders in our church called me on a Monday morning to schedule a meeting. I had no idea what he wanted to meet about, but by the tone of his voice, I felt like I was being called to the principal's office. As he sat down in my office, his first words were, "Pastor, we've got a problem." I listened and tried to refrain from becoming defensive as he continued. "Yesterday, you said Jesus is God." He looked at me as if waiting for me to admit I had misspoken.

I honestly did not remember making that statement and tried to quickly analyze if this was a trick question. After a matter of moments, I said, "I don't remember saying that, but I believe that."

He rebutted, "Jesus cannot possibly be God . . . why would He pray to himself?" His statement was shocking to me. He was in his seventies, had been the primary adult class teacher for years, and was an influential board member in our church.

His issue was something I had never doubted. Until that time, I assumed that Jesus' deity is a basic Christian belief and that all Christians understand Jesus is, in fact, fully God. I was wrong. This man never could grasp how Jesus could have been born fully God and fully man. He considered my theology heretical. However, Jesus' deity is a foundation of Christian theology. The Apostle John began his Gospel with this proclamation:

> *In the beginning was the Word, and the Word was with God, and the Word was God. He was in the beginning with God. All things were made through him, and without him was not anything made that was made. And the Word became flesh and dwelt among us, and we have seen his glory, glory as of the only Son from the Father, full of grace and truth.* (John 1: 1-3, 14)

In other words, Christ has existed from before creation and has been involved in every aspect of the story of humanity since time began.

Every Christmas most of us hear, or sing, the song by Charles Wesley, *Hark! The Herald Angels Sing* (1739).

> *Christ, by highest Heaven adored; Christ the everlasting Lord; Late in time, behold Him come, Offspring of a virgin's womb. Veiled in flesh the Godhead see; Hail the incarnate Deity, Pleased with us in flesh to dwell, Jesus our Emmanuel! Hark! the herald angels sing, "Glory to the newborn King!"*

> Jesus is one hundred percent God and one hundred percent man.

Jesus' birth heralded the prophesied incarnation, *Immanuel*, God with us. Jesus is one hundred percent God and one hundred percent man. Difficult to grasp? Yes! Yet our faith is full of concepts that are incomprehensible to us. The incarnation, the concept of being eternal, and the concept of the trinity are each perplexing. Even devout believers have a difficult time understanding how someone or something can be one hundred percent one thing and one hundred percent another. Despite our bafflement, Jesus is completely man and completely God.

And because Jesus is fully God and fully man, His birth was not His beginning. It merely represented the physical manifestation of God in the flesh. Jesus is eternal. The concept of being eternal is also difficult to grasp. We have no real, tangible example or frame of reference for understanding eternity. Jesus has always existed. He has no beginning, and He has no end. Jesus is eternally God. Jesus was not only there at the creation of the world, but John proclaims Jesus was the actual creator!

Jesus was born as God with us so He could pay the price for our sins and bring us into the eternal Kingdom of God. He was born of a virgin, lived a sinless life, died on the Cross, was buried, and rose on the third day.

Following His resurrection, 1 Corinthians 15:6 tells us Jesus appeared to more than five hundred people. He taught His followers about the Kingdom of God and told them He would send the Holy Spirit to empower them as His witnesses. Acts 1:9 says that Jesus was taken up into a cloud and ascended into Heaven while His followers watched until they could no longer see Him. As they gazed, awestruck at His disappearance into the clouds, perhaps they reflected on what Jesus had told them.

Present: Jesus *Is* God with Us!

Jesus, the eternal creator of the world, became God with us. He made His home among humanity, and once His mission was complete, He went away. His followers surely had to wonder, "God *with* us is now God gone *from* us?" But then, I am sure they remembered His words:

> *"I did not say these things to you from the beginning, because I was with you. But now I am going to him who sent me, and none of you asks me, 'Where are you going?' But because I have said these things to you, sorrow has filled your heart. Nevertheless, I tell you the truth: it is to your advantage that I go away, for if I do not go away, the Helper will not come to you. But if I go, I will send him to you. . . . When the Spirit of truth comes, he will guide you into all the truth, for he will not speak on his own*

authority, but whatever he hears he will speak, and he will declare to you the things that are to come." (John 16:4-7, 13)

Is Jesus now God gone from us? At times, it may appear that way. But that is not what Jesus taught. He told His disciples it was necessary for Him to go away so that He could send the Spirit of Truth, the Comforter, the Counselor, the Empowerer. While Jesus walked this earth in the flesh, He could only be in one place at one time. He knew His followers needed more. They would be dispersed throughout the world and their numbers would grow to the degree that a single human being would be unable to be with each person as he, or she, needed.

> Jesus' plan was to fully engage in the lives of each of His followers throughout all time.

Jesus' plan was to fully engage in the lives of each of His followers throughout all time. He could do that only by ascending into Heaven and sending His Spirit. We know Jesus as the Holy Spirit. Like Jesus, and the Father, the Holy Spirit is eternally God. The Holy Spirit is God with us in spirit form, right here and right now. He lives in the hearts of every believer, and He desires to fill us to overflowing. He empowers us, guides us, and gives us the correct words to say when we have absolutely no idea what to say. The Holy Spirit is God with us.

We have come to know the three manifestations of the Godhead—the Father, Son, and Holy Spirit—as the Trinity. *Trinity* is not a term found in the Bible, but it is a Biblical concept. Matthew 28:19 says that believers are to "go and make disciples of all nations, baptizing them in the name of the Father and the Son and the Holy Spirit." In other words, we are to share the message of the Trinity.

The Father, Son, and Holy Spirit are each distinct personalities who make up one complete whole. Like the word *eternal*, the Trinity is a difficult concept for us to grasp. Again, we have no real, tangible frame of reference to help us adequately understand it. Many have concocted analogies to try and help us understand the Trinity. For example, some liken the Trinity to water. Water can take the form of liquid, solid (ice), and a gas. Yet, in each state it is still conceivably water. Others have used the example of a light bulb. A light bulb is a physical bulb, which produces both light and heat. These examples help us to begin to understand the concept of the Trinity, but as most analogies, they eventually break down and are inadequate.

Because the Trinity is such a difficult concept to grasp, there are those who say Christians believe in three Gods. That is categorically false. The

Christian faith is monotheistic. We believe in one God. Our founder, Jesus, taught that there is one only God.

In Mark 12:29, Jesus says, "Hear, O Israel: The Lord our God, the Lord is one." This statement, known as the *Shema*, is one of the most important phrases in the Jewish prayer. It is the proclamation that there is only one God. Jesus prayed this and Jesus believed this. Why, then, would His followers adopt a three-God faith? There is only one God, and we understand God to be manifest in three distinct personalities, the Father, the Son, and the Holy Spirit.

In order for Jesus to accomplish His promise found in Matthew 28:20, "I am with you always, even to the end of the age," He had to ascend into Heaven. He is now within us and beside us! In 1 Corinthians 6:19, the Apostle Paul writes, "Or do you not know that your body is a temple of the Holy Spirit within you, whom you have from God?" Jesus is still alive and seated at the right hand of God the Father in Heaven. He is interceding for us (Romans 8:34) and His Spirit is dwelling within us!

With that indwelling of the Holy Spirit in each believer, the Church should be bound together by unified guidance in one mission. The Apostle Luke wrote, in Acts 1:1-8,

In the first book, O Theophilus, I have dealt with all that Jesus began to do and teach, until

the day when he was taken up, after he had given commands through the Holy Spirit to the apostles whom he had chosen. He presented himself alive to them after his suffering by many proofs, appearing to them during forty days and speaking about the kingdom of God. And while staying with them he ordered them not to depart from Jerusalem, but to wait for the promise of the Father, which, he said, "You heard from me; for John baptized with water, but you will be baptized with the Holy Spirit not many days from now."

So when they had come together, they asked him, "Lord, will you at this time restore the kingdom to Israel?"

He said to them, "It is not for you to know times or seasons that the Father has fixed by his own authority. But you will receive power when the Holy Spirit has come upon you, and you will be my witnesses in Jerusalem and in all Judea and Samaria, and to the end of the earth."

And yet despite the clarity of this mission to be witnesses throughout all the world, one of the greatest divisions in modern Christianity is the divergent doctrines of the Holy Spirit. This rift grieves God's heart. He sent His Spirit to empower us and to unite us. Instead, sometimes we turn the Spirit into something to debate and divide over!

> Jesus prayed for His disciples,
> including you and me, before He was
> arrested in the garden.

Jesus prayed for His disciples, including you and me, before He was arrested in the garden. John 17 shows Jesus praying that we would be one, just as He and the Father are one. His Spirit not only empowers us but lives in each of us, uniting us as brothers and sisters.

I have had the privilege of traveling extensively. I love exploring new places and making new friends around the world. One thing that never ceases to amaze me is that when I meet a fellow believer anywhere in the world, we are immediately family—even if we don't speak the same language. How can this be? It is unnatural; it is supernatural. This brotherhood can only be attributed to the common Spirit living in every believer. In a very real sense, the Spirit of God living in the people of God is another means of Jesus being with us to the ends of the age!

Historically, Jesus was God with us when He walked this earth, and Jesus is God with us in the present through His Spirit who lives in all believers. But wait, that is not yet the end of the story!

Future: Jesus *Will Be* God with Us!

We have already looked at Acts 1 and Jesus' ascension, but let's put this passage in its full context.

> *"But you will receive power when the Holy Spirit has come upon you, and you will be my witnesses in Jerusalem and in all Judea and Samaria, and to the end of the earth."*
>
> *And when he had said these things, as they were looking on, he was lifted up, and a cloud took him out of their sight. And while they were gazing into heaven as he went, behold, two men stood by them in white robes, and said, "Men of Galilee, why do you stand looking into heaven? This Jesus, who was taken up from you into heaven, will come in the same way as you saw him go into heaven."* (Acts 1:8-11)

This passage is so encouraging because it is a confirmation that Jesus will return! The Jews waited a long time for the coming of a Messiah. At just the right time, God sent His Son. We have now waited a long time for the return of the Messiah, but at just the right time, God will send Him again!

We find this promise repeated in the final words of the Bible:

> *"He who testifies to these things says, 'Surely I am coming soon.' Amen. Come, Lord Jesus! The grace of the Lord Jesus be with all. Amen."* (Revelation 22:20-21)

> The entire story of Scripture ends
> on this promise of hope—
> He is coming back.

The entire story of Scripture ends on this promise of hope—He is coming back.

Jesus also spoke of His return in the Gospel of John.

"Let not your hearts be troubled. Believe in God; believe also in me. In my Father's house are many rooms. If it were not so, would I have told you that I go to prepare a place for you? And if I go and prepare a place for you, I will come again and will take you to myself, that where I am you may be also. And you know the way to where I am going."

Thomas said to him, "Lord, we do not know where you are going. How can we know the way?"

Jesus said to him, "I am the way, and the truth, and the life. No one comes to the Father except through me." (John 14:1-6)

Think back to the event I shared with you at this beginning of this chapter. My wife and I asked for help in finishing the basement of our house because we were preparing our home and lives for our child coming to join us. Christ mirrors this beautiful picture of what He is doing, right now, in heaven—

preparing for all of His children to join Him! And we know that someday He will throw open the doors of heaven and run out to meet us, ushering us into our home that He has prepared for our arrival.

Since the days of the Early Church, Jesus' followers have been looking forward to His return. There were some early believers who apparently stopped working and simply sat around waiting for Jesus to come back and rapture them from this life. This was a significant enough issue that the Apostle Paul wrote to the Christians of Thessalonians (2 Thessalonians 3:6) to stay away from those who didn't work.

I have been a Christian since I was seven years old. From the beginning, I remember people talking about Jesus' return. Very elderly people have told me they have heard all their lives that Jesus is coming soon. In fact, the first-generation Christians expected He would return in their lifetimes. As evidenced clearly in children, patience tends to be a struggle for humans. It is easy to become cynical, to stop looking for His return, and to even stop really believing Jesus will return at all.

The concept of Jesus' return is foundational to Christian doctrine, and we cannot stop looking to the clouds. If Jesus lied about coming back, then how can we trust anything He said? If we remember the concept of being eternal, that there is no beginning or end to God, we will remember that to

Him a day is like a thousand years. Do not become disillusioned, He will come again! Consider the Apostle Peter's encouragement to some believers of the Early Church:

> . . . knowing this first of all, that scoffers will come in the last days with scoffing, following their own sinful desires. They will say, "Where is the promise of his coming? For ever since the fathers fell asleep, all things are continuing as they were from the beginning of creation." For they deliberately overlook this fact, that the heavens existed long ago, and the earth was formed out of water and through water by the word of God, and that by means of these the world that then existed was deluged with water and perished. But by the same word the heavens and earth that now exist are stored up for fire, being kept until the day of judgment and destruction of the ungodly.

> But do not overlook this one fact, beloved, that with the Lord one day is as a thousand years, and a thousand years as one day. The Lord is not slow to fulfill his promise as some count slowness, but is patient toward you, not wishing that any should perish, but that all should reach repentance.

> But the day of the Lord will come like a thief, and then the heavens will pass away with a roar, and the heavenly bodies will be burned up and dissolved, and the earth and the works that are done on it will be exposed.

Since all these things are thus to be dissolved, what sort of people ought you to be in lives of holiness and godliness, waiting for and hastening the coming of the day of God, because of which the heavens will be set on fire and dissolved, and the heavenly bodies will melt as they burn!

But according to his promise we are waiting for new heavens and a new earth in which righteousness dwells."

(2 Peter 3:3-13)

The creator of the world is also the creator of time. So, to Him, time does not function as we experience time. The long days and years of waiting for us are simply a blink of an eye to Him as He finishes putting into place the final pieces necessary to the preparation of His return and the new glory ahead.

Jesus *was* God, He *is* God, and He always *will be* God. He is the same yesterday, today, and tomorrow. The fact that God himself willingly clothed himself in flesh, gave His life, sent His Spirit to live in us, and promised to return for us is a great testament to His love.

God has always loved you.
God loves you now.

God always will love you!

Reflect . . .

1. Have you ever had someone come alongside you when you needed help? How did that make you feel?

2. What does, "Jesus Christ is the same yesterday, today, and forever" (Hebrews 13:8), mean to you? How does this fact impact you?

3. In what ways does Jesus' presence with you, right here and right now, comfort and encourage you?

4. How does knowing Jesus will come again influence your living today?

Chapter 3
The Greatest Gift

"Greater love has no one than this, that someone lay down his life for his friends."

John 15:13

Every year my wife asks me, "What do you want for your birthday?" She knows the question is somewhat rhetorical because the answer is almost always, "Nothing." One year, early in our marriage, she believed me. When September 14 came, we went to dinner, and she handed me a card. I opened it and there was nothing inside except a brief note and her signature. I waited for her to bring out the present after we ate.

On the way home, I thought to myself, "Oh, it was too big to bring to the restaurant, so she'll give it to me at home." Once home, she started doing the laundry. Later that evening she noticed something was wrong with me, so she inquired. I told her I was a little hurt that she didn't get me a present. She quickly repented and begged for forgiveness. Jumping in her car, she sped straight to the store to get me a present . . . *NOT!* The truth is we had a very *robust* conversation about how unfair I was to tell her I wanted nothing and then expect her to get me something.

The reason I can never think of what I want for my birthday is that I have this habit of just buying whatever I want (within reason, of course). If I want a pair of shoes, I get them. If I need a bottle of wax for my car, I get it. I like to shop, so I am never really in need of much. However, this habit does leave my wife, and now my kids, with a dilemma every year on my birthday.

In buying my own presents, I miss the opportunity for my family to show me their love and appreciation. Giving is a way we can demonstrate our love and affection to others. Gifts don't have to be purchased; even a handmade gift can have a great cost of thought, time, and energy.

In fact, my greatest treasures are the gifts my kids make themselves. We often correlate the level of affection we receive from someone with the cost of the gift they give us. A painting that took ten minutes to complete does not seem to demonstrate the same level of affection as a painting that took months, like one my oldest son gave me. That is a costly gift even though no dollar price was attached. We simply cannot give gifts like that to ourselves!

Great Cost Demonstrates Great Love

Out of all the gifts given throughout all the history of humankind, one gift stands in a class of its own as the costliest: the gift of love as demonstrated by Jesus through His death on the cross. This gift was given to all people. This gift was given to you.

> *"Greater love has no one than this, that someone lay down his life for his friends. You are my friends if you do what I command you. No longer do I call you servants, for the servant does not know what his master is doing; but I have called you friends, for all that I have heard from my Father I have made known to you. You did not choose me, but I chose you and appointed you that you should go and bear fruit and that your fruit should abide, so that whatever you ask the Father in my name, he may give it to you. These things I command you, so that you will love one another."* (John 15:13-17)

Not only does this passage tell us about the love Jesus has for you, it also reveals what Jesus thinks about you—you are His friend!

Jesus Loves You and Gave His Life for You!

In Chapter 1, we discussed how God covered Adam and Eve's nakedness with an animal sacrifice. Throughout the Scriptures, we read of the sacrificial system implemented as a temporary payment for sin. The spilling of the blood of an innocent animal was a foreshadowing of the Cross where the Son of God would offer the ultimate sacrifice as the payment of the penalty of sin. This sacrifice was the final payment for the sins of anyone who will acknowledge and receive this great gift. The gift of Jesus laying down His life is for you.

> The gift of Jesus laying down His life is for you.

It is easy for us to think of Jesus dying for a world of people, but it is sometimes difficult to fully grasp the fact that Jesus laid down His life for you and me as individual people. There is an old Gospel song that says, "While he was on the cross, I was on his mind." Jesus' life sacrifice was a personally crafted gift—for you.

The Apostle Paul, in 1 Corinthians 6:19-20 writes, "Do you not know that your body is a temple of the Holy Spirit who is in you, whom you have from God, and that you are not your own? For you have been bought with a price." That *price* was Jesus' life, and greater love has no man than he who lays down his life for his friends!

Jesus Chose You!

In John 15:16, Jesus explains that we did not choose Him, but He chose us. When I read this passage in context, I understand that Jesus is directly speaking to His disciples—the ones He chose. But as I step back, I see He was really speaking to all people; and all people includes you and me!

Can you fathom the extraordinary mystery of why God would choose you? I know I have great difficulty understanding why God would choose to send His only son to die on a cross for me. Why would He choose to have a relationship with someone like me? I certainly haven't earned it, and I sure don't deserve it. And yet that very mystery is the beauty of God's love. His love is underserved, and it is unearned!

> When we refused to choose to love Him, He chose to love us.

While we were still living in our sin, Jesus willingly laid down His life for us. When we refused to choose to love Him, He chose to love us. He chose us before time literally began!

> . . . *even as he chose us in him before the foundation of the world, that we should be holy and blameless before him. In love he predestined us for adoption to himself as sons through Jesus Christ, according to the purpose of his will.*" (Ephesians 1:4-5)

In choosing us, Jesus made us a part of His family. Once we accept His sacrificial gift of love, we are adopted as children of God! 1 John 3:1 (NIV) declares, "See what great love the Father has lavished on us, that we should be called children of God! And that is what we are!" We are God's adopted children—who He deems as worthy of His name.

I once had the opportunity to sit with a family who had an adopted child. This child had reached an age where she began to recognize she didn't look like her parents. Her skin and hair color were different than her mom, dad, and her siblings. Her parents knew it was time to tell her she had been adopted. However, they were not quite sure how to approach the topic. They asked me to help navigate the conversation. During the meeting, the mother said to the adopted child, "We love you as much as we love your brother and your sister. We didn't give birth to you like we did to them, but we love you just as much. In fact, we didn't have a choice in having your brother and your sister, but we chose you! Out of all the little boys and girls in the world who do not have a mother and daddy, we chose you! That's how much we love you!"

The young girl's eyes lit up and a big smile formed on her little face. The thought of being specially chosen gave her a new perspective, and I am confident it transformed her life! Once you grasp that you have been chosen by God, your life becomes transformed.

> Once you grasp that you have been chosen by God, your life becomes

The Gift of the Cross: Because You Matter to God

You are loved, you are chosen by God, and He has a plan for you! 1 Peter 2:9 affirms that we are chosen, that we are a royal priesthood, and that we are holy; and furthermore, our mission from God is to point others to Jesus. God loves you so much that He has entrusted you with declaring His praises. That means that He has entrusted you to make sure the world knows about the same great, mysterious love you have received!

Later, we will dive deeper into God's plan for us, but for now, recognize that Jesus sees you as someone worth dying for, choosing, and endorsing to carry His name and His mission to the world. What a great honor!

The Gift of the Cross: A Thread Woven through History

For Christ did not send me to baptize but to preach the gospel, and not with words of eloquent wisdom, lest the cross of Christ be emptied of its power.

For the word of the cross is folly to those who are perishing, but to us who are being saved it is the power of God. For it is written, "I will destroy the wisdom of the wise, and the discernment of the discerning I will thwart."

Where is the one who is wise? Where is the scribe? Where is the debater of this age? Has not God made foolish the wisdom of the world?

For since, in the wisdom of God, the world did not know God through wisdom, it pleased God through the folly of what we preach to save those who believe. For Jews demand signs and Greeks seek wisdom, but we preach Christ crucified, a stumbling block to Jews and folly to Gentiles, but to those who are called, both Jews and Greeks, Christ the power of God and the wisdom of God. (1 Corinthians 1:17-24)

For the Apostle Paul, the cross of Jesus was the seminal event in all human history. It is the foundation of the Christian faith, and it is a prominent thread woven throughout the Old and New Testaments. To cover Adam and Eve's sin, an animal was sacrificed; to provide temporary forgiveness for the sins of the people of Israel, animals were sacrificed; and at the command of God, Abraham was willing to sacrifice his son, Isaac, as a sin offering. All these events foreshadowed the coming of a spotless Lamb of God—Jesus the Messiah—who was the ultimate and final sacrifice for sin.

> The Cross is our lifeline to God.

The Cross is our lifeline to God. Because of the Cross, we have uninterrupted access to God. There is a constant nagging voice for many pastors, including me, to come up with a novel, unique, and insightful sermon each week, but Paul was committed to ONE thing: the Cross of Jesus. Sure, he taught about other things, but the heart of all he taught was Jesus crucified. This message isn't redundant, antiquated, or irrelevant. The Cross is the power of God that brings salvation to everyone who believes (Romans 1:16).

The Gift of the Cross: Foolish to Some and Life to Others

"For the word of the cross is folly to those who are perishing, but to us who are being saved it is the power of God."

(1 Corinthians 1:18)

The words of Jesus continually confounded the wise and taught a philosophy contrary to conventional wisdom.

His statements like, "To find your life, you must lose it," and, "The first will be last," are examples of Jesus' upside-down teachings. Perhaps the best example is found in Matthew 5:3-12, the Sermon on the Mount.

Blessed are the poor in spirit, for theirs is the kingdom of heaven. Blessed are those who mourn, for they shall be comforted. Blessed are the meek, for they shall inherit the earth. Blessed are those who hunger and thirst for righteousness, for they shall be satisfied. Blessed are the merciful, for they shall receive mercy. Blessed are the pure in heart, for they shall see God. Blessed are the peacemakers, for they shall be called sons of God. Blessed are those who are persecuted for righteousness' sake, for theirs is the kingdom of heaven. Blessed are you when others revile you and persecute you and utter all kinds of evil against you falsely on my account. Rejoice and be glad, for your reward is great in heaven, for so they persecuted the prophets who were before you.

Our world teaches that the strong inherit the best, and those willing to push their way forward are those who succeed and earn recognition. Such nonsense Jesus' teachings can seem at first glance.

The Cross similarly turns everything upside down. What we perceive as wisdom is foolishness to God. There is no sense to the idea that God would come in the flesh and sacrifice His own life to give us life.

The Greeks were philosophers, and they chased wisdom and knowledge. Celsus, a Greek philosopher and early Christian opponent, said:

> *God is good, and beautiful, and blessed, and that in the best and most beautiful degree. But if he come down among men, he must undergo a change, and a change from good to evil, from virtue to vice, from happiness to misery, and from best to worst. Who, then, would make choice of such a change? It is the nature of a mortal, indeed, to undergo change and remolding, but of an immortal to remain the same and unaltered. God, then, could not admit of such a change.* (Congregation for the Clergy, 2020)

So why would God do such a thing? Why would He choose such a drastic measure? Because of love! The Cross is foolishness to the Greek, and even to many modern day people, including some philosophers and academics. But God did not wait for the Cross to make sense to us. Romans 5:8 says,

> *God demonstrates his love for us, in that in while we were still sinners, Christ died for us.*

Notice that God took action "while we were still sinners." Jesus didn't wait until we were ready or good enough. He went ahead to the Cross and did what we could never achieve ourselves

The Gift of the Cross: Our Access to God

A commercial for a mobile phone carrier popularized the phrase, "Can you hear me now?" In the commercial, a person would be speaking on a mobile phone and lose reception. He or she would then move from location to location, trying to find reception, repeating the phrase, "Can you hear me now?"

When Adam and Eve disobeyed God, sin entered the world and broke the reception between humans and God. Our relationship with God was fractured and we were alienated from God. Throughout the Scriptures, the sacrifice of animals temporarily brought reconciliation between God and humanity. But those sacrifices were impermanent—duct tape to a leaking pipe. Jesus' gift of the Cross brought permanent reconciliation between humans and God, restoring full reception in our communication with God.

As Jesus breathed His last breath, He cried out in a loud voice and surrendered His spirit to the Father. At that moment, the temple curtain was torn from top to bottom (Matthew 27:50-51). The veil in the temple is symbolic of the barrier between man and God, and at the time of the temple in Jesus' day, the curtain stood about 60 feet high. The fact that the curtain was torn from top to bottom symbolizes it was an act of God and not anything a human could have done.

This symbolism was so profound that God chose not only to tear the veil but also to record it in the Bible for all history. He clearly desires for us to know we have direct access to Him because of the gift of the Cross.

The Gift of the Cross: God's Love Demonstrated by Grace

My family and I once lived near an active train track. When we first moved to that home, we were regularly distracted by the sound of the whistle as the train passed through the intersection near our house. After a few months, I realized I was no longer bothered by the sound of the train. In fact, I hardly even noticed it. This phenomenon is known as familiarity blindness—when we become so familiar with something that we no longer consciously see it. Familiarity blindness affects us all.

For some readers, all this talk about God's love may seem redundant. Why would I spend so much time writing about God's love? The reason is that some readers may be learning of God's love for the first time; and for all of us, my prayer is that we will see God's love as if for the first time. It is easy for us to experience familiarity blindness with God's love. Those who regularly attend church hopefully often hear about God's love. We all need to hear about God's love, but we need to be careful to not become immune to its power.

> It is easy for us to experience familiarity blindness with God's love.

Grace is another word we may often hear about. Grace is closely related to love. Because of God's love, He gives us grace. Grace is simply getting what we do not deserve and what we have not earned. 1 Corinthians 1:4-5 says, "I always thank my God for you because of his grace given you in Christ Jesus." In other words, churches and Christian community only exists because God gave each of us what none of us deserves—love, forgiveness, and a restored relationship with Him. Don't allow yourself to be blinded in familiarity to the incredible gift of the Cross.

The Gift of the Cross: God's Grace, Not Our Works

When we first come into a relationship with Jesus, grace is all we have. We are excited that God has given us life, even when we don't deserve it. Then, many begin what I term as a "grace substitution" cycle. Another description of this could be legalism or rule following. This cycle begins because Christians experience familiarity blindness to God's grace. Ephesians 2:8-9 reminds us all that "It is by grace [we] have been saved, through faith—not by works, so that no one can boast." We must never forget that our works did not make us good enough for God, Jesus did it all in His gift of the Cross.

I have watched new Christians revel in God's grace, and in their excitement, share that grace and love with others. As they mature, they recognize God wants them to become more like Jesus. Human nature is to analyze, so in our analysis, many of us will make a list of the characteristics Jesus possesses and begin striving to attain those qualities. The motivation is pure, but with that focus, we can change from desiring to become like Jesus to simply pursuing a quality. There is a subtle and dangerous distinction between these two focal points. We will address this distinction in more detail in later chapters, but for now the point is to remember it is God's grace that saves us not our works.

The Gift of the Cross: God's Mercy Wins!

The Old Testament lists about 613 laws. There are so many laws we would never be able keep them all. These laws create an impossible standard to which we cannot measure. So why would God create such an impossibility of living? The laws are there to demonstrate we need help . . . we need God! God is a holy God—a perfect being. We can never live our lives in such a way as to be perfect enough to be accepted into His presence. The multitude of laws is a small demonstration of the type of exact perfection we would have to live by in order to try to perfect ourselves before God. Impossible to do!

> We can never live our lives in such a way as to be perfect enough to be accepted into His presence.

The punishment for lawbreaking was severe. Numbers 15:32-36 gives an example.

While the people of Israel were in the wilderness, they found a man gathering sticks on the Sabbath day. And those who found him gathering sticks brought him to Moses and Aaron and to all the congregation. They put him in custody, because it had not been made clear what should be done to him. And the Lord said to Moses, "The man shall be put to death; all the congregation shall stone him with stones outside the camp." And all the congregation brought him outside the camp and stoned him to death with stones, as the Lord commanded Moses.

The punishment for breaking the Sabbath was stoning. That seems a severe punishment for picking up a few sticks on the wrong day. However, in Romans 6:23, Paul tells us the payment for our sin—all sin—is death, but the gift of God is eternal life in Jesus.

Sin is simply missing the target, and we have all missed the target. Whether by a lot or a little, the consequence of missing the target is eternal death. Harsh judgment? Yes. But we're talking about a perfectly holy God. Because God loves us so much, He enacted a strict measure and severe punishment to demonstrate His grace. We must understand His judgment to appreciate His grace!

Jesus said, in Matthew 5:17, that He did not come to do away with the Law but to fulfill it—to the pay the price of sin. Jesus is God's grace and mercy in action, and "mercy triumphs over judgment" (James 2:13).

God's gift of the Cross is the greatest gift anyone could ever give, and it is the greatest gift anyone could ever receive. But a gift, to have purpose, must be received. Have you received this great gift? If so, do you find yourself entering a grace substitution cycle, trying to follow rules and perform for God's love?

We can never fulfill the Law, so Jesus did it for us through His death. In Galatians 2:21, Paul says that he does not dismiss God's grace because, if right-standing with God could be gained through obeying the Law, then Jesus' death was worthless. Remember this: We are made right with God by His grace, not by our goodness!

> Remember this: We are made right with God by His grace, not by our goodness!

Reflect . . .

1. What is the greatest gift you have ever received? Who gave you that gift?

2. What made the gift so great?

3. What was the occasion?

4. Was the gift costly in time, energy, or perhaps in the thought that went into choosing it? How did it make you feel?

5. Have you received God's gift of salvation?

Chapter 4
Lost and Found

"For the Son of Man came to seek and to save the lost."

Luke 19:10

When visiting a city for the first time, I have a talent for ending up in the worst part of town. On my first visit to Brussels, Belgium, I spent a couple of days in a hotel near the city center. I love to explore, so I began walking. I passed a beautiful cathedral and ended up in the Grand Place, one of Europe's most beautiful city centers. I continued walking and eventually left the tourist district. I remember the sinking feeling and the surge of adrenaline as I realized, "I am lost!"

Some young men huddled in a small group near an alley. One by one, they turned to watch me as I walked by. Avoiding eye contact, I stood up tall, squared my shoulders back, and rallied my best Clint Eastwood scowl as I fixed my gaze ahead of me. My pace quickened as if I were a man on a mission. I took the first turn I suspected would get me headed in the direction of my hotel. Nothing looked familiar and my heart pounded more quickly. As I made another series of turns, I stumbled across a familiar landmark. I breathed a heavy sigh of relief. My pace and my pulse slowed as I stopped to take a quick rest. There is nothing like the feeling of knowing you're lost and then being found.

> There is nothing like the feeling of knowing you're lost and then being found.

Jesus captures this distinctive sensation when He tells a beautiful story in Luke 15:3-7:

So he told them this parable: "What man of you, having a hundred sheep, if he has lost one of them, does not leave the ninety-nine in the open country, and go after the one that is lost, until he finds it? And when he has found it, he lays it on his shoulders, rejoicing. And when he comes home, he calls together his friends and his neighbors, saying to them, 'Rejoice with me, for I have found my sheep that was lost.' Just so, I tell you, there will be more joy in heaven over one sinner who repents than over ninety-nine righteous persons who need no repentance."

The story of the lost sheep is not only beautiful because the sheep is rescued but because the shepherd rejoiced so greatly in its return. Do you understand that God wants you to be found, not just for your sake, but because of the joy you bring Him?

God knows we are lost before we recognize it ourselves. He created us to be in relationship with Him, and when that relationship is broken, we wander the streets of life seeking something, anything, that will fill the hole in our heart. Because God loves you and me so desperately, He made the ultimate sacrifice to ensure we had a way home, and then He sent His Spirit to search for us. He knows we cannot find our way home by ourselves, so He set out to find us, His lost sheep.

The shepherd's love for the lost sheep is obvious. He left the many who were safe to find that one sheep. You are that one sheep. I am that one sheep. You and I matter to the Shepherd! He rejoices when we are found!

How do I Fill this Hole in my Heart?

Many wander the streets of life not realizing they are lost. Often haunted by a nagging feeling of emptiness, they long for more. Humankind was banished from the Garden of Eden because of sin. We were exiled from home, from the presence of the loving God who created and sustained us, and left to drift through life longing to be reconnected to our source.

The feeling of empty longing, known as *object hunger* by psychologists, is universal. We search for satisfaction in substances, relationships, possessions, finances, accomplishments, charity work, and even religion. Relief from the emptiness is always fleeting, except when found in a relationship with God. Someone who has never experienced the fulfillment found in a relationship with God will likely wander from object to object seeking the wholeness for which they desperately long.

Along our journey, God strategically places road signs and landmarks. We may not recognize them as such, but God desires to gently lead us home. He desires to be found, but He also wants us to desire to find Him. Jeremiah 29:11 assures of God's good plan for our lives, but the next few verses are equally inspiring, especially when we consider they were written to God's people who were lost, searching for hope, on a long journey home from captivity in Babylon. Jeremiah 29:11-14 says:

> *"For I know the plans I have for you," declares the LORD, "Plans for welfare and not for evil, to give you a future and a hope. Then you will call upon me and come and pray to me, and I will hear you. You will seek me and find me, when you seek me with all your heart. I will be found by you," declares the LORD, "And I will restore your fortunes and gather you from all the nations and all the places where I have driven you, declares the LORD, and I will bring you*

back to the place from which I sent you into exile."

God has a good plan for your life, and that plan is integrally connected to finding Him! If you have not found God yet, He is waiting for you. He is ready to be found. In all your searching for fulfillment, ask Him to reveal himself to you. Seek Him and He will be found. Then you, the banished, will be brought home from exile. 2 Samuel 14:14 tells us, God "devises ways so that a banished person does not remain banished from him." Imagine that. He devises ways for you to be brought home!

> God has a good plan for your life, and that plan is integrally connected to finding Him!

Even those who find God sometimes wander off. A hymn written by Robert Robinson (1758), *Come Thou Fount of Every Blessing*, says, "Prone to wander, Lord, I feel it, Prone to leave the God I love." I can identify with that statement. Although God satisfies my emptiness, my human nature continually compels me to seek more. Like Adam and Eve, I am tempted to want more than God provides even while I know that the things God does not provide are not provided because they are destructive to me. It doesn't make sense, but as the

Apostle Paul identifies, it is a war continually waging inside of me (Romans 7).

I have to remember I am a work in progress. When I've wandered down a street in curiosity, or in rebellion, I must become increasingly aware of the warning signs the Holy Spirit places along the way. God knows our battles. He knows our natural desire to explore satisfaction in the fleeting validation of the world.

Hebrews 12:6 says that God disciplines those He loves. *Discipline* is a word I dislike. I haven't met many people who like to be disciplined. It is often associated with punishment. However, God's discipline is always redemptive. His discipline acts as a warning sign to guide us back to the path leading to Him. God desires relationship with you. Whether you have never met Him, or you have met Him and wandered away, His arms are open, and He calls out to you, "Here I am, come home to me!"

How Do I Enter a Relationship with God?

You have seen the verse on cardboard signs in the end zones of NFL games and on billboards by the interstate. Children around the world memorize it: "For God so loved the world that he gave his one and only Son, that whoever believes in him shall not perish but have eternal life." John 3:16 is likely the most beloved and well-known verse in all the Bible.

Why? Because it captures the essence of God's heart. God loved and God gave. Think about it. God loved the world. This includes every person who has ever lived and ever will live, including you. That is a lot of people!

God's ultimate plan of entering relationship with you and me was to offer His one and only son, Jesus, as a sacrifice to pay the price for our sin. Because He loves us, He went to great extremes and demonstrated outrageous love to make sure we had every opportunity to know Him. Jesus' sacrifice paid the price of admission into God's Kingdom and into relationship with Him. You and I were created for this relationship with God, and that is what we have been aching for all our lives.

So just how do we enter that relationship? In Acts 16:30-31, the Apostle Paul and Silas were asked, "Sirs, what must I do to be saved?" They replied, "Believe in the Lord Jesus, and you will be saved." Their response echoes John 3:16 that whoever believes in Jesus shall not die but have eternal life.

Believing in Jesus is not the same as believing in the president of the United States. It is not a simple acknowledgement of His existence or even believing what He says is true. It is a faith-filled knowing on which believers build their lives. The Apostle Paul stated that we are saved by grace through faith in Jesus. This salvation has nothing to do with what we have or have not done; this is so that we can't take the credit. Salvation is purely a gift from God (Ephesians 2:8-9).

> Believing in Jesus and coming to Him through faith is both simple and complex.

Believing in Jesus and coming to Him through faith is both simple and complex. It costs us both nothing and everything. In its simplicity, we simply come to Him, believing Jesus is God's son, that He was born in the flesh, lived a sinless life, gave His life as a sacrifice for our sin, and rose again on the third day. He lives today and gives life to you and to me.

In our more modern tradition, becoming a Christian, or Christ-follower, has often been reduced to repeating a simple prayer which usually goes something like this:

Dear Jesus, I confess my sin to you, and I receive your sacrifice on the Cross as payment for my sin. Thank you for loving me and thank you for washing me clean. I choose to follow you, and I commit my life to you. In Jesus' name, Amen.

I often invite people to pray a prayer like this at the end of a church service, and I have prayed similar prayers with individuals I have helped enter a relationship with Jesus. It is a good prayer, but our relationship with God only begins here.

How Do I Grow in My Relationship with God?

Too often, people have desired to enter a relationship with Jesus only to be led to pray that prayer and then be left to figure out the rest on their own. Every relationship begins at some point, but if it never progresses in intimacy past the introduction, that relationship will not develop. You will not truly know the other person and the other person cannot truly know you.

You can know God intimately just as you get to know anyone intimately: by spending time with Him. When we spend time with people, we speak, we listen, we observe, and we naturally begin to take on some of their attributes. In spending time with God, we pray, read the Bible, and bring our lives into alignment with the teachings of the Bible. Speaking to God is known as prayer. Jesus taught His disciples how to pray:

> *Our Father in heaven, hallowed be your name, Your kingdom come, your will be done, on earth as it is in heaven. Give us this day our daily bread, and forgive us our debts, as we also have forgiven our debtors. And lead us not into temptation, but deliver us from evil.* (Matthew 6:9-13)

In this model prayer, Jesus is teaching His disciples how to talk to the Father. He did not intend for us to recite this prayer as a ritual, rather to give us an example. Other examples in the Bible demonstrate there is not a special formula for prayer; however, prayer will usually incorporate some form of honoring or worshiping God, asking Him to let you know His will for you and accepting that His will be done, and requests for any needs you or others may have. Prayer also includes repentance and asking for forgiveness of sin.

Speaking to God is a vital part of prayer and a vital part of building intimacy with Him. However, if we do all the talking when we are with a friend, how can we get to know them? How can they communicate with us? I am a talker, and I must intentionally remind myself to let others talk when we are together, not only because it is a nice thing to do, but if I genuinely care about another person, I will listen.

> Getting to know someone requires listening.

Getting to know someone requires listening. God speaks to us through the Bible and through the Holy Spirit. In the Bible, we can learn about God's character, His desire for us, and we can learn from the teachings and the lives of the authors and other biblical characters. God still speaks through the Bible because it is a living document, inspired and illuminated by God's Spirit.

> *For the word of God is living and active, sharper than any two-edged sword, piercing to the division of soul and of spirit, of joints and of marrow, and discerning the thoughts and intentions of the heart.* (Hebrews 4:12)

When we read the Bible, we are learning about the very heart of God. And as we learn about God, His Word becomes our mirror, and we learn to examine ourselves through His eyes and His character.

God also speaks to us through the Holy Spirit. Jesus told His followers (and us) He would be leaving this earth, but He would send His Spirit to be in us and with us. The Holy Spirit guides, comforts, counsels, gives us words to say to others, and empowers us to live the life God desires for us to live. He speaks to our hearts directly.

Jesus said His sheep know His voice. By listening, we learn to hear the Spirit of God over time. Psalm 46:10 says, "Be still and know that I am God." When we are quiet, we give God the opportunity to speak to us, and He generally speaks in a still small voice.

> As with any relationship, we must be intentional about communication with God.

As with any relationship, we must be intentional about communication with God. Many voices regularly compete for our attention. Each day we are bombarded with marketing techniques, books telling us how to live, and experts giving us self-help tools to achieve our full potential. No one is exempt from the many voices vying for attention. Even pastors are continually marketed books, conferences, workshops, and programs designed to help their churches grow. Often the loudest and most creative voices garner attention and consequently are heard. Some of the voices are good, but as Jim Collins (2001) says, "Good is the enemy of great" (p. 1).

Books on spiritual formation, self-help, and leadership, for example, are generally good information and helpful; however, none should take priority over God's Word, the Bible. As the latest, greatest books are released with a flurry of marketing and attention, the Bible often sits unobtrusively on the shelf, quietly proclaiming, "This is the way . . . walk in it" (Isaiah 30:21).

Knowing + Doing = Growing

Overstating the importance of the Bible in the life of a Christian is impossible. God placed high value on Scripture and went to great lengths to produce and preserve His Word for you and for me.

Consider what went into the production of the Bible: sixty-six books, forty authors, written over a 1,500-year span. I have friends who have co-authored books. It takes great planning and diligence to ensure continuity in flow, style, and content. Think of the true miracle it took to create a single book written over 1,500 years by forty authors—all with different personality styles, writing styles, perspectives, personal agendas—producing a congruent story of God and His relationship with humankind!

The Bible is another example of the great love God has for you and for me. The Bible has been called the greatest love story ever written... and it truly is. The Bible is the story of how God loves first. As we read of His love for us, we are inspired to love Him more. The more we love God, the more we desire to become like Him.

> We grow to look more like Jesus by spending time with Him in His Word.

We grow to look more like Jesus by spending time with Him in His Word. As a teen, I was regularly reminded of the power of peer pressure. The important adults in my life recognized that the more time I spent with a person or a group of people, the more I begin to act like and bear a resemblance to them.

King Solomon said that when we walk with a wise person, we become wise, but if we walk with fools, we suffer harm. (Proverbs 13:20) Greek dramatist, Euripides wrote in his play, *Phoenix*, "Every man is like the company he keeps." In modern times, many have been attributed with the statement, "Show me your friends and I'll show you your future." By spending time with God in prayer and in His Word, we begin to be transformed into His image. We begin to become the man or woman we were created to be, and we begin experiencing a fulfilled life—a life of knowing we, who were lost, have been found! And when we have been found by God, He rejoices as a shepherd who found a lost sheep!

The Psalmist wrote, "I have stored up your word in my heart, that I might not sin against you" (Psalm 119:11). King David loved God's Word, mediating on it, and memorizing it. But he didn't stop there. He stored it up in his heart so that it could impact his behavior. God's Word is not simply great literature; it is, as the writer of Hebrews says, "alive and active"! (Hebrews 4:12)

Merely hearing what God is saying to us through His Spirit and through His Word is not enough. We must act on it. "Do not merely listen to the word, and so deceive yourselves. Do what it says" (James 1:22, NIV). In Matthew 7:24-27, Jesus tells a story about a man who built his house on the sand and another who built his house on a rock. Sometimes we read this passage and think we simply need to build our house on Jesus or perhaps His Word. However, Jesus clearly states that the one whose house is built on the rock is the one who hears God's words *and* does them. Knowing what God says in His Word is important for a Christ-follower, but without acting on them, those words are not transformative.

Knowing God's Word helps us know who God is and learn what He expects from us. Doing God's Word, putting it into practice, develops Christ-like character within us.

Knowing + Doing = Growing!

You and I were lost, and Jesus went on a search and rescue mission to find us. Once He found us, He provided a way for us to have relationship with Him and to develop depth in that relationship. His love for you and His love for me drove Him to seek us out. He didn't wait for us to find Him.

He didn't wait for us to become good enough.

He went searching for us despite our brokenness and how lost we had become.

He loved first!

Reflect . . .

1. Have you ever been lost? How did you feel?

2. How did you react when you were found or found your way to safety?

3. In what ways has Jesus demonstrated that He has searched for you?

4. Has God used people in your life to find you? Who and how?

Chapter 5
Everyone Walks with a Limp

But God showed his great love for us by sending
Christ to die for us while we were still sinners.

Romans 5:8 (NLT)

My father died when I was eight years old.
While my mother did eventually remarry, the hole
left by my dad's passing seemed bottomless. My
grandfather and I had always been close, and I
began to look to him as my father figure. He owned
a gas station, had horses, and was a calf roper. He
even bought me my first horse when I was two
years old. As a child, I spent hours washing
windows and filling gas tanks at my granddad's
service station. I idolized him.

My granddad had a reputation for helping
people in need. In the days before twenty-four-hour
pumps, gas stations closed each evening. Late one
night, a family with an ill child drove through our
little West Texas town on the way to the hospital in
Lubbock. They found the sheriff's department and
inquired where they might get fuel. The sheriff
called my granddad. He immediately got dressed
and went to his station. My granddad then filled the
family's tank for free. He was a good man. In my

eyes, he was almost perfect. But he, too, was broken.

In trying to cope with losing my dad, his youngest son, my granddad began self-medicating with alcohol. His drinking deeply and negatively impacted my family and me. One night he could not cope any longer and, in front of my grandmother, put a pistol to his temple and pulled the trigger. His suicide shattered my world and destroyed my family. For the second time the most important man in my life had been taken.

> When a boy loses his dad at a young age, he spends the rest of his life seeking his approval.

It has been said that when a boy loses his dad at a young age, he spends the rest of his life seeking his approval. Well, I had now lost my dad and my grandfather. From that time on I looked to others for approval and affirmation. I performed my best and pursued academic degrees, success, and material things. With each accomplishment, I received affirmation from others I respected, but it never seemed to be enough. On the outside I was successful, yet on the inside, I was a child longing to hear his dad say, "Good job, son. I am proud of you."

Everyone Has a Story. Everyone is Broken.

Everyone has a story. Everyone is broken. Many people live their lives searching for answers to questions still unknown—wandering from experience to experience, relationship to relationship, and substance to substance—attempting to find the answer to the longing inside. From the most successful entrepreneur to the man who lives by donations in a cup, we all make our way through this life with a limp even though some live through extraordinarily difficult situations while others appear blessed with a golden touch like the Greek mythological King Midas.

My heroes are those who prevail over adversity, achieving success and significance. Appearing to possess a special success gene, these men and women reach great levels of influence and make impressive contributions to the world. Personally meeting my heroes always thrills and often sobers me. Without fail, I find them to be individuals simultaneously worthy of honor and broken. Which fact should actually be an encouragement to us all—you are not alone; I am not alone. Everyone is broken. We all walk with a limp.

> We all walk with a limp.

We find the root of our brokenness in the story of Adam and Eve in the Garden. Each of us carries an emptiness in our soul, a longing for satisfaction. And nothing on this earth seems to permanently satisfy. Sure, we may find temporary gratification in accomplishments, substances, or relationships, but eventually we hunger and thirst again. I know this hunger and thirst intimately from my long chase after the illusive satisfaction of approval.

Like me, have you walked through life with a limp? Are you longing for something you cannot quite identify? Do not despair; your limp is coded into your DNA! Because God actively loves you and me, He placed within us a hunger and thirst that can only be satisfied by reclaiming what we lost in the Garden.

> When the cool evening breezes were blowing, the man and his wife heard the LORD God walking about in the garden. So they hid from the LORD God among the trees. Then the Lord God called to the man, "Where are you?"
>
> He replied, "I heard you walking in the garden, so I hid. I was afraid because I was naked."
>
> "Who told you that you were naked?" the Lord God asked. "Have you eaten from the tree whose fruit I commanded you not to eat?"
> (Genesis 3:8-11, NLT)

God asked, "Where are you?" The implications of this simple question resound with relationship! This whole scene reminds me of coming home from work and based on previous experience, fully expecting to be greeted by my spouse. When this doesn't happen, I immediately call out, "Honey, where are you?" The big difference is God knew exactly where Adam and Eve were.

In this passage, God asks three questions: "Where are you?" "Who told you that you were naked?" "Have you eaten from the tree whose fruit I commanded you not to eat?" Interesting questions for an all-knowing God, don't you think? Yet these questions were not asked for God's sake but to begin a dialogue.

After they sinned, Adam and Eve hid. They saw their nakedness and were ashamed. Very clearly God did the pursuing in this relationship, and He still does. Adam and Eve were broken; they now walked with a limp. God could have erased them and started over. But He didn't. He loved them. He loved them first. While their disobedience had consequences, God continued to love and provide.

But everything changed. Intimacy and peace between God and man shattered. Peace between Adam and Eve shattered. And peace between man and the rest of creation shattered into countless broken pieces.

*Therefore the Lord God sent him [Adam] out
from the garden of Eden to work the ground
from which he was taken. He drove out the man,
and at the east of the garden of Eden he placed
the cherubim and a flaming sword that turned
every way to guard the way to the tree of life.*
(Genesis 3:23-24)

God's Cosmic Scheme

Thus began the story of humanity's limp, a story fraught with toil and struggle. We live constantly striving to be good enough, to do the right thing, and yet always fall short. We are born in exile from the Garden, in exile from intimacy with God, and with the emptiness of longing sewn into our DNA. Before man's great fall, God would come to the Garden in the cool of the day and spend intimate time with His creation. I am reminded of a Gospel song written by C. Austin Miles (1913) called, "In the Garden." The chorus says:

*And he walks with me, and he talks with me,
And he tells me I am his own;
And the joy we share as we tarry there,
None other has ever known.*

This song captures the essence of the intimacy with God for which we were created! Is there anything in this world that can compare? Because of sin, we are left out in the cold, separated from God, but our innermost being knows the satisfaction and warmth of a real relationship with the Father, and we long for it. God longs for this intimacy as well. From the beginning of our limp, God has given assistance, providing ways to restore us into fellowship with Him.

> *We must all die; we are like water spilled on the ground, which cannot be gathered up again. But God will not take away life, and he devises means so that the banished one will not remain an outcast.*
> (2 Samuel 14:14)

God devises ways to return a banished person from exile!

God devises ways to return a banished person from exile! Because God loves us, He schemes to give us a way back to Him. In the Old Testament, we read of sacrifices providing temporary forgiveness for sin. In Jesus, we find God clothing himself in flesh and coming to Earth. In Jesus, we find an echo of the Garden—God walking, once again, with humankind. In Jesus, we find God loving first.

> *In this the love of God was made manifest among us, that God sent his only Son into the*

world, so that we might live through him. In
this is love, not that we have loved God but that
he loved us and sent his Son to be the
propitiation for our sins... We love because he
first loved us.
(1 John 4:9-10, 19)

Jesus put on flesh so we might experience abundant
and eternal life. Longing, hunger, and thirst give
way to satisfaction. Why? In Jesus, we find God's
ultimate scheme to bring the banished person out of
exile and into relationship! Jesus fulfills in us every
area in which we fall short. He makes us in *right*
standing with God or, to use the biblical word,
righteous.

The Psalmist wrote, "Because I am righteous, I
will see you. When I awake, I will see you face to
face and be satisfied" (Psalm 17:15, NIV). We can
never come to God through our own
accomplishments or goodness. It is only by
receiving Jesus' sacrifice that we can stand in
righteousness. Yet that righteousness is not ours but
His, and because His righteousness satisfies the
price for our sin, our relationship with God is
restored. And in that restoration, we reclaim what
we lost in the Garden: the irreplaceable satisfaction
of a truly intimate relationship with God.

Who Moves First?

Jesus invites us to come, to eat the bread of life and drink the living water that fully satisfies. But how do we come? A survey by LifeWay Research found:

> *Two out of three Christians (68%) said that a person obtains peace with God by seeking God first, and then God responds with grace. A similar percentage (67%) said people have the ability to turn to God on their own initiative. Yet half (54%) also think salvation begins with God acting first.* (Emmert, 2014)

So just how do we get from here to there? Who makes the first move?

This theological debate goes back centuries. Pelagius, a British monk in the fifth century, believed people could come to God on their own will. Based on the LifeWay statistics, Pelagius was not alone. Was Pelagius correct? Are two out of three Christians correct? Why does this question even matter? Who cares who makes the first move as long as someone makes the first move?

These sorts of theological and doctrinal questions are subjects often left to academia. Many Christians and pastors do not appreciate the importance of having good theology and biblical doctrine. *Theology* is simply the study of God. *Doctrine* is a set of beliefs. Biblical theology and doctrine help us to understand who God is, how He interacts with people, and what He expects of us. Our understanding of who makes the first move is a foundational assumption in our theology and doctrine.

The most credible source from which to explore the answer to our question is God's Word.

> *"No one can come to me unless the Father who sent me draws him. And I will raise him up on the last day."* (John 6:44)

This passage in John is an important statement by Jesus. Here He clearly says that God is the initiator of our faith. The Greek word translated as "draw" is *helkuo*, which means literally or figuratively "to drag." John 21 tells how Jesus' disciples went fishing all night and caught nothing. At sunrise, Jesus stood on the shore and told them to cast their nets on the right side of the boat. They caught so many fish they were unable to haul them all in! The same Greek word as Jesus used in John 6:44, *helkuo,* is used in this passage for *haul or drag.* Very clearly, the Father, through the Holy Spirit, is the one who draws, or in some cases drags, us to Jesus! He takes the first step!

Who Does All the Work?

So, we've established Jesus steps first. But what about the next steps? What role do we play? The same LifeWay research also revealed, "More than half of survey participants (55%) said people have to contribute to their own salvation" (Emmert, 2014). Again, we find a majority of professing believers with a skewed understanding of biblical doctrine. The Bible is clear that God has expectations of those who profess to believe, but we very clearly find that we make absolutely no contribution to our salvation and standing with God.

The letter written by James has long been a source of controversy in the New Testament. James spoke so highly of works, the way we live and the things we do, that Martin Luther wanted the entire book of James excluded from the Bible. Martin Luther's reaction against a works-oriented belief system is understandable, but James never stated that works are a requisite for salvation.

James does state, "Faith by itself, if it is not accompanied by action, is dead" (James 2:17). Reading this verse in context, we find James is simply saying faith is demonstrated by action. An inward knowing will result in an outward doing. Do we have to work for our salvation, or can we earn any part of our salvation? No and no.

The Apostle Paul addressed this question head-on.

> *For by grace you have been saved through faith. And this is not your own doing; it is the gift of God, not a result of works, so that no one may boast.* (Ephesians 2:8-9)

> *I do not nullify the grace of God, for if righteousness were through the law, then Christ died for no purpose!* (Galatians 2:21)

In these passages, Paul boldly declares God's grace as the sole provision for our souls. Yes, we all walk with a limp. We are broken, empty, and longing for something more—longing to reclaim what we lost in the Garden. But what comfort we find in knowing God has always been there. He has always schemed and devised ways to ensure that we, who were banished, would not have to stay out in the cold.

God's ultimate plan in sending Jesus was to pay the final price for our sin.

God's ultimate plan in sending Jesus was to pay the final price for our sin. A payment, when accepted, covers over all our brokenness, all our sinfulness, and makes us in right standing with God. His Spirit draws us, perhaps even drags us, to find

Him and to receive the wonderful gift of life. All because of His amazing grace—all because of His amazing love—the broken is now made complete and whole.

A New Storyline

We are all broken. We all walk with a limp. The Apostle Paul describes us as being everyday dishes as opposed to fine china! *The Message* paraphrase describes our state like this:

> *If you only look at us, you might well miss the brightness. We carry this precious Message around in the unadorned clay pots of our ordinary lives. That's to prevent anyone from confusing God's incomparable power with us.* (2 Corinthians 4:7)

Yes, you and I are clay pots . . . chipped, cracked, and ordinary. However, once the presence of God fills these pots, the ordinary becomes extraordinary! The light of God can shine through our cracks, making us a vessel of extreme value and beauty.

If we were beautiful in and of ourselves, we would be tempted to let our light and beauty be the center of attention. However, recognizing we are vessels carrying within us the glory of God, we are overjoyed to shine for Him. Our story is transformed and woven into His story!

Everyone has a story. Everyone begins his or her story broken, walking with a limp. But because God took the initiative, because God loved first, our storylines can take a new direction. A person whose story looked hopeless is now full of hope and potential. A person whose story was without purpose is now full of meaning. A person whose story was full of abandonment and pain is now embraced with full acceptance. Stories can change. People can change. You and your story can change.

Do not be defined by your past experiences, you are a part of God's eternal story... and your story has a happy ending!

Reflect . . .

1. Reflect on your life story. In what ways might you "walk with a limp?"

2. How has your limp impacted your life?

3. Have you entered into relationship with Jesus? When did you meet Him?

4. How can you see God reaching out to you throughout your life?

5. How has becoming a follower of Jesus influenced your storyline?

Chapter 6
The Children of God

*See what kind of love the Father has given to us,
that we should be called children of God; and
so we are.*

1 John 3:1a

Everyone has a story. Our stories are formed from our individual perspective of life-events, what we tell the world about who we are, and what others say about us. These stories are sometimes inconsistent, and they are always interpreted differently by the people around us. Unfortunately, often the story we believe and tell others about who we are is incongruent with the story the Bible tells about who we are.

Each of our stories takes a dramatic turn when we understand our identity as a Christ-follower. The Apostle John tells us that God generously poured out His love on us and made us His children (1 John 3:1-2).

> Everyone has a
> story.

In this passage, I love the word the translators of the New International Version used instead of *poured: lavished.* The Merriam-Webster Dictionary defines *lavish* as, "expending or bestowing profusely." To lavish something is luxurious and elaborate. God did not just *give* us His love, He *lavished* His love on us!

When someone becomes a child of God, their story is impacted at a cellular level. As the Apostle Paul writes in 2 Corinthians 5:17, the old you is dead! The old story is over! A new story begins when a believer begins a new life. That new life comes with privileges and responsibilities.

The Gospel of John (chapter 3) tells how a religious leader named Nicodemus came to Jesus at night. Obviously, Jesus had gotten his attention and he had questions about Jesus' teachings, specifically about how to enter the kingdom of God.

Jesus told Nicodemus it is impossible to enter the Kingdom unless a person is *born again.* This phrase has been adopted by Christians since the Early Church for describing the act of choosing to become a follower of Jesus. When someone accepts Jesus' sacrifice on the Cross as payment for their sin and places their trust in Him as their savior and king, they go through the spiritual process of being reborn.

But to all who did receive him, who believed in his name, he gave the right to become children of God, who were born, not of blood nor of the will of the flesh nor of the will of man, but of God. (John 1:12-13)

As a believer, you are born again, not by flesh and blood, as you were physically born, but by the Spirit of God. You are born into God's family as a son or daughter.

Just as in your biological birth, you are not born mature but like an infant who must grow and develop. 1 Peter 2:2 compares new Christians to newborn babies and encourages all Christians to long for the pure milk of the Word. By God's Word, we can grow into mature Christ-followers! This growing in respect to salvation is a joint process of our discipline and God's transforming Spirit.

By God's Word, we can grow into mature Christ-followers!

The Consequences of Being a Child of God

Persecution

Let's get this one out of the way first. Jesus said to His disciples that they would be hated by all because of their relationship with Him (Matthew 10:22-23). That is a strong statement and to take it literally would be to misunderstand what Jesus meant. Jesus was divisive when He walked on this earth, and He is divisive today. When people don't fully comprehend the love of God and why Jesus came, they look at Him and His followers as judgmental and selective. Some say they can't believe in a God who would allow suffering, and some despise the fact that Christianity teaches eternal life or that there is only one way to heaven.

Persecution is one of the consequences of being a Christ-follower. Consider the following passages:

> *For this reason the world does not know us is that it did not know Him.* (1 John 3:1)

> *"And you will be hated by all for my name's sake. But the one who endures to the end will be saved. When they persecute you in one town, flee to the next, for truly, I say to you, you will not have gone through all the towns of Israel before the Son of Man comes."* (Matthew 10:22-23)

> *"Remember the word that I said to you: 'A servant is not greater than his master.' If they persecuted me, they will also persecute you. If they kept my word, they will also keep yours."* (John 15:20)

Persecution shouldn't come as a shock to us. Jesus warned His followers that they would be mistreated and even killed. According to Church tradition, this is how some disciples died: Matthew was killed with a sword in Ethiopia; Mark was dragged through the streets of Alexandria; Luke was hanged upon an olive tree in the land of Greece; Peter was crucified at Rome with his head pointed downward; James the Apostle was beheaded at Jerusalem; James the brother of Jesus was thrown from the pinnacle of the temple and then beaten to death with a club.

Persecution didn't end when the Apostles passed from the scene. Sadly, it continues to this day. Around the globe Christians are being martyred and persecuted for their faith in Jesus. This is terrible and we should pray for our brothers and sisters who are suffering such persecution. But we have hope! Jesus said,

> *In the world you will have tribulation. But take heart; I have overcome the world. (John 16:33)*

Provision

I have two sons. Both are now adults, but they will always be my little boys. I love them unconditionally and overwhelmingly. They carry my name, but more than that, they carry my undying devotion, care, and compassion. I would give my life to protect them. Jesus talked about earthly fathers as compared to the Heavenly Father (Matt 7:11). If I care for my kids that much and I am imperfect, how much more does the perfect Heavenly Father care for His children? Because God lavishly loves you, you can be confident in His provision for you.

God's provision does not always look as we think it should or want it to look. We all have preconceptions about what is best for us and what God should do to provide for us. However, as with any child, sometimes the wisdom of the parent is better than the wants of the child.

As an all-knowing God, our Father can place our lives in context of the whole, not just the moment or the season. In 1990, country music superstar, Garth Brooks, recorded a song with the line, "Sometimes I thank God for unanswered prayers." He told how he and his wife went back to their hometown and attended a high school football game. As the song says, he realized that the prayer he had prayed in high school went unanswered. He had dreamed of marrying a particular young lady and that relationship ended. Back then, I am sure he was devastated, but in time, he realized God had a better plan for him. I can identify with that song, and I am sure you probably can as well.

> Trusting God with our lives
> is a process.

Have you ever longed for God to open a specific door, maybe for a job, education, or other opportunity? At the time, you just know this is the right move . . . but the door doesn't open. Sometimes we can look back and say, "Thank you,

God, for not answering that prayer with a 'yes.'"
Other times we may not see the purpose, but God
does. Trusting God with our lives is a process. It
becomes easier as we grow in relationship with
Him. You can have confidence that whatever your
need, God is good, and He cares for you. As Jesus
said in Matthew 6, the Father cares for the birds of
the air, how much more will He care for you?

God provides for our earthly needs, but He also
provides for our spiritual needs. While we walk this
earth, He has promised to provide His Holy Spirit to
guide us, comfort us, teach us, and empower us. We
can entrust our lives to Him, both now and for
eternity.

God knows what is best for us, and even when
we do not like His answer, we continually discover
that He was right. God's provision may not look
like what we want it to look like, but God is always
good to His children. He will always do what is best
for us and for His Kingdom. As we mature in our
relationship with God, we begin to trust Him more
and more.

Discipline

As any earthly parent disciplines his or her
children, so does God the Father. As Hebrews 12
tells us, God disciplines us because He loves us. No
one likes to be disciplined. It seems unpleasant at
the time, but discipline has an important role. One

of the key components of healthy and loving discipline is that it is always geared toward restoration and transformation rather than harsh punishment. In other words, healthy discipline is restorative and not punitive.

Without discipline, we do not learn, and we do not grow. We know that God not only disciplines, but He also encourages. For example, when Jesus was baptized, God said, "This is my beloved Son, with whom I am well pleased" (Matt 3:17). Jesus told a story about how a master, representing God the Father, praised a faithful servant, saying, "Well done, good and faithful servant" (Matthew 25:21). Our goal, as children of God, is to receive this good report; however, when we need it, God is also there to lovingly guide us through restorative discipline. In this way, we can grow up in our faith and take on the family resemblance of looking and acting like Jesus.

Transformation

Attaining this family resemblance is really our goal in this lifetime. God is daily molding and shaping us into the image of Jesus.

As I mentioned earlier, my father died when I was young. Several years later, when I was a young teenager, we went to visit my hometown. My grandmother and I went to the grocery store; the woman who checked us out looked at me, having never seen me before, and said, "You are Bruce's boy, aren't you?"

Surprised, I said, "Yes." She went on to tell me how I looked like him, I walked like him, and I had the same mannerisms as he had. That was an important and affirming moment for me.

My prayer is that when others see me, they can say, "You're God's boy, aren't you?" It may take a lifetime, but what a testimony to the transformational work of the Holy Spirit in my life if others are able to see the Father in me!

As children of God, you and I can be confident there will be repercussion for our faith in the form of persecution. However, we can also be certain of the ultimate victory! As children of God, you and I can also be confident of God's provision, His discipline, and our progressive transformation.

As a child of God, you have been adopted into God's family because He took the initiative and loved you first!

Reflect . . .

1. How does understanding that you are a child of God impact your identity?

2. What are some of the ways you have experienced the consequences of being a child of God?

- Persecution

- Provision

- Discipline

- Transformation

- Other ways?

3. In what ways can you see the family resemblance you may have with Jesus?

Chapter 7
You are the Temple of God

Don't you realize that your body is the temple of
the Holy Spirit, who lives in you and was given
to you by God? You do not belong to yourself,
for God bought you with a high price.

1 Corinthians 6:19-20a (NLT)

I had just finished dinner on a cold and dreary
Sunday evening in London. Too early for bed and
too late to shop, I decided to attend the evening
service at one of the most prominent landmarks in
the city. As I entered the massive Westminster
Abbey, I was overwhelmed by a sense of God's
majesty that inspired such an elaborate worship
facility. But I was equally underwhelmed by the
fifty or so seats which had been arranged for the
few of us in attendance. A massive church which
easily could have accommodated thousands of
people was virtually empty. The United Kingdom
and Europe are full of stunning, ancient cathedrals
and churches. Sadly, many of them are more
museums than thriving communities of believers.
Perhaps more heart-breaking are the ones converted
to theatres, restaurants, and bars.

A cathedral is a building created to provide a
place for worshipers to connect with God.

Unfortunately, they can sit virtually empty, unfulfilling the intended purpose of their creators. As followers of Jesus, we have been created for specific purposes, as well. The Apostle Paul says that we are temples of the Holy Spirit.

> *Don't you realize that all of you together are the temple of God and that the Spirit of God lives in you? God will destroy anyone who destroys this temple. For God's temple is holy, and you are that temple. . . . Don't you realize that your body is the temple of the Holy Spirit, who lives in you and was given to you by God? You do not belong to yourself, for God bought you with a high price. So you must honor God with your body.* (1 Corinthians 3:16-17;19-20, NLT)

There are two Greek words translated as "temple" in the New Testament: *hieron* and *naos*. *Hieron* refers to the entire temple complex while *naos* refers to only the Holy Place and the Holy of Holies. *Naos* is used in Matthew 27:51 when referring to the curtain in the sanctuary of the temple that was torn in two, from top to bottom. Can you guess which one of these Greek words Paul uses in 1 Corinthians? *Naos*! You are the Holy Place, the Holy of Holies, the place where the presence of God dwells!

The temple was vital to the Jewish people. The concept of the temple was based upon the pattern of the Tabernacle from when Moses led the Israelites out of slavery in Egypt. It was a place of sacrifice and worship. The temple represented where the presence of God lived. The study of the Jewish temple reveals remarkable history as well as a rich foreshadowing of God's ultimate desire to dwell, not only *among*, but *within* His people.

> The temple represented where the presence of God lived.

The Building of the Original Temple

The original temple, built by Solomon, the son of King David, was completed in 939 BC. 2 Chronicles tells us

Then Solomon began to build the house of the Lord in Jerusalem on Mount Moriah, where the Lord had appeared to David his father, at the place that David had appointed, on the threshing floor of Ornan the Jebusite. He began to build in the second month of the fourth year of his reign. These are Solomon's measurements for building the house of God: the length, in cubits of the old standard, was sixty cubits, and the breadth twenty cubits. The vestibule in front

of the nave of the house was twenty cubits long,
equal to the width of the house, and its height
was 120 cubits. He overlaid it on the inside with
pure gold. The nave he lined with cypress and
covered it with fine gold and made palms and
chains on it.   (2 Chronicles 3:1-5)

Paying special attention to the materials and craftsmanship, Solomon constructed the first extravagant house of worship. He began with giving meticulous care to the foundation. He used fine gold as an overlay and adorned the temple with precious stones.

The temple's dedication was unlike anything ever seen before. Countless animals were sacrificed, and the priests sang and played instruments in worship. Then the presence of God descended like a cloud, and the cloud was so great the priests had to stop what they were doing!

This original temple was destroyed 400 years later by the Babylonians only to be reconstructed again in 516 BC. Then Rome's Pompey destroyed the temple yet again in 62 BC only to have it rebuilt by Herod the Great, a process which took from 20 BC to 64 AD. This version of the temple is the one that stood when Jesus first started His ministry. This temple was again destroyed in 70 AD by the Romans and has not been rebuilt since that time. Don't overlook the significance of this last destruction of the temple. After all, the temple was designed to be a representation of where God lived. But with the coming of Christ, that representation has completely changed—Christ followers are now the temple.

Let's look again at the context of what the Apostle Paul says, taking into consideration the construction and history of Solomon's temple:

> *According to the grace of God given to me, like a skilled master builder I laid a foundation, and someone else is building upon it. Let each one take care how he builds upon it. For no one can lay a foundation other than that which is laid, which is Jesus Christ. Now if anyone builds on the foundation with gold, silver, precious stones, wood, hay, straw— each one's work will become manifest, for the Day will disclose it, because it will be revealed by fire, and the fire will test what sort of work each one has done. If the work that anyone has built on the foundation survives, he will receive a reward. If anyone's work is burned up, he will suffer loss, though he himself will be saved, but only as through fire.*
>
> *Do you not know that you are God's temple and that God's Spirit dwells in you? If anyone destroys God's temple, God will destroy him. For God's temple is holy, and you are that temple.* (1 Corinthians 3:10-17)

Throughout history, the presence of God was separated from His people, but on the day Jesus gave His life, the curtain that separated the Holy of Holies was torn from top to bottom as if by God himself. Prior to Jesus' sacrifice, only the High Priest could enter the Holy of Holies. The ripping of the curtain represents God throwing open the door to His presence for all who trust in Jesus! You and I are invited to approach Him in confidence.

> *Because of Christ and our faith in him, we can now come boldly and confidently into God's presence.* (Ephesians 3:12, NLT)

> *So let us come boldly to the throne of our gracious God. There we will receive his mercy, and we will find grace to help us when we need it most.* (Hebrews 4:16, NLT)

Because of Jesus' payment for our sin and the filling of His Holy Spirit, we have become the dwelling place for God. You are the temple of God, the house of God . . . He lives in you! Just as Solomon took special care in building his temple on a firm foundation, God built His new temple on a firm foundation—the foundation of Jesus. The furnishings of our temple are not gold or precious stones but are the lives we live and the glory we bring to God.

You are the temple of God, the house of God . . . He lives in you!

God Has Always Desired to be With Us

In Genesis, we find Adam and Eve hiding from God in the garden when He came to visit in the cool of the day. Their sin changed everything. The relationship between humans and creation and the relationship between humans and God had been severed. God's presence could no longer dwell freely among humankind. God quickly made a covering for Adam and Eve, but the consequences of their choice remained. We find God, throughout the Scriptures, meeting with people for a temporary time but never truly dwelling among them. With the institution of the Tabernacle and then the Temple, we find God's presence dwelling among men but still separated from them. Yet God has always desired to be with us.

The Apostle John writes that when Jesus came to this earth, the Word, Jesus, became flesh and made His dwelling among us. However, we rejected Him. Upon His death, the curtain was torn from top to bottom, symbolizing that the way had been permanently opened for God to truly dwell, not just among His people, but within His people.

When the Holy Spirit was given to the disciples (Acts 2), we find the overwhelming presence of God flooding the upper room, not unlike the glory of God in the dedication of Solomon's Temple.

What follows are the accounts of these two events; the similarities are stunning.

Dedication of the Temple:

> *When Solomon finished praying, fire flashed down from heaven and burned up the burnt offerings and sacrifices, and the glorious presence of the LORD filled the Temple. The priests could not enter the Temple of the LORD because the glorious presence of the LORD filled it. When all the people of Israel saw the fire coming down and the glorious presence of the LORD filling the Temple, they fell face down on the ground and worshiped and praised the LORD, saying, "He is good! His faithful love endures forever!"* (2 Chronicles 7:1-3, NLT)

Day of Pentecost:

> *On the day of Pentecost all the believers were meeting together in one place. Suddenly, there was a sound from heaven like the roaring of a mighty windstorm, and it filled the house where they were sitting. Then, what looked like flames or tongues of fire appeared and settled on each of them. And everyone present was filled with the Holy Spirit and began speaking in other languages, as the Holy Spirit gave them this ability.* (Acts 2:1-4, NLT)

Notice how the presence of God, the Holy Spirit, filled both places, how He manifested himself in the form of fire, and how the response of the people was verbal.

God has always desired to be with His people, and in filling us with His Holy Spirit, He is with us in a very intimate way! The presence of God is now poured out on all who would place their trust in Jesus. God's presence is dwelling with humankind once again. More accurately, God's presence is dwelling *within* humankind. The need for a building to house the presence of God has become obsolete. His people are now the temples of His presence. The Holy Spirit is at home in you and me. What an astonishing concept.

> *"If you love me, obey my commandments. And I will ask the Father, and he will give you another Advocate, who will never leave you. He is the Holy Spirit, who leads into all truth. The world cannot receive him, because it isn't looking for him and doesn't recognize him. But you know him, because he lives with you now and later will be in you. No, I will not abandon you as orphans—I will come to you. Soon the world will no longer see me, but you will see me. Since I live, you also will live... All who love me will do what I say. My Father will love them, and we will come and make our home with each of them."* (John 14: 15-19, 23, NLT)

God's Home is a Holy Place

In the dedication of the temple and on the day of Pentecost, fire played a prominent role. Was it because fire would get the attention of the people? I know it would get mine. But there is more. Fire represents a purification process. Here is what the Bible tells us about the fire of God:

> *"I will bring that group through the fire and make them pure. I will refine them like silver and purify them like gold. They will call on my name, and I will answer them. I will say, 'These are my people,' and they will say, 'The Lord is our God.'"* (Zechariah 13:9, NLT)

> *The Lord your God is a devouring fire.* (Deuteronomy 4:24, NLT)

> *He will sit like a refiner of silver, burning away the dross. He will purify the Levites, refining them like gold and silver, so that they may once again offer acceptable sacrifices to the Lord.* (Malachi 3:3, NLT)

> *For our God is a devouring fire.* (Hebrews 12:29, NLT)

> *These trials will show that your faith is genuine. It is being tested as fire tests and purifies gold—though your faith is far more precious than mere gold.* (1 Peter 1:7, NLT)

God is holy and His holiness will consume anything that isn't holy. *Holy* simply means "set apart for a purpose, dedicated, and different." As with much of our walk with God, the concept of being holy is a "now and not yet" process.

> In placing our faith in Jesus, we are immediately made holy and acceptable to God.

In placing our faith in Jesus, we are immediately made holy and acceptable to God. Our sins are forgiven, and we can come into God's presence with boldness, not because we have done anything to make us worthy but because Jesus' sacrifice makes us worthy. 1 Peter 2:9 tells us, "You are a chosen people. You are royal priests, a holy nation, God's very own possession" (NLT). Did you understand that? *You* are chosen, a royal priest, and holy!

We are holy now and we are also being made holy as we continue to walk with God. When the Holy Spirit dwells in us, we are continually being refined and purified to become more like Jesus. The process of becoming holy, or more like Jesus, is called *sanctification*.

But we ought always to give thanks to God for you, brothers beloved by the Lord, because God chose you as the first fruits to be saved, through sanctification by the Spirit and belief in the truth. (1 Thessalonians 2:13)

You are God's temple, His dwelling place, having been made holy and being refined and made continually holy through the work of the Holy Spirit in you.

What amazing and lavish love God has poured out on us! Not only has He given us eternal life, but He has also chosen to make His home within us.

While God makes His home within us because of His love and His grace, we still have a responsibility to live as the temple we are blessed to be. 1 Peter 2:9 tells us that we are called out of darkness into His light, that we may demonstrate His praises—that we may shed light on the dark world around us. 1 Peter 1:15-16 (NLT) says, "But now you must be holy in everything you do, just as God who chose you is holy. For the Scriptures say, 'You must be holy because I am holy.'" Being holy is a command.

So, God makes us holy at conversion, continues to make us holy by His Spirit, and we have a responsibility to practice holiness! As Solomon's temple was dedicated to God, so are we to be dedicated and set apart to God.

The Temple is Dear to God's Heart

Following the dedication of the temple, God appeared to Solomon and said:

> *I have heard your prayer and have chosen this Temple as the place for making sacrifices. At times I might shut up the heavens so that no rain falls, or command grasshoppers to devour your crops, or send plagues among you. Then if my people who are called by my name will humble themselves and pray and seek my face and turn from their wicked ways, I will hear from heaven and will forgive their sins and restore their land. My eyes will be open and my ears attentive to every prayer made in this place. For I have chosen this Temple and set it apart to be holy— a place where my name will be honored forever. I will always watch over it, for it is dear to my heart.* (2 Chronicles 7: 12-16, NLT)

The temple was "dear to God's heart." What an odd statement. The temple was a building constructed by human hands—a building that would eventually be destroyed. What made this building dear to His heart? It was not the extravagance of the temple but rather because it represented the place He could dwell among the people He loved. The temple was a demonstration that the people God loved cared enough to give their best to Him. The temple was dear to God's heart because of love.

How much more does God love you? You are a creation of His own hands. You are designed to live through eternity with Him even after the earthly tent has been destroyed. You are more than a physical body; you are a soul infused with the very presence of God. You are the temple; you are the dwelling of God. You are dear to God's heart, and He promises He will always watch over you!

> You are dear to God's heart, and He promises He will always watch over you!

The Temple is a House of Prayer

Jesus entered the Temple and began to drive out all the people buying and selling animals for sacrifice. He knocked over the tables of the money changers and the chairs of those selling doves. He said to them, "The Scriptures declare, 'My Temple will be called a house of prayer,' but you have turned it into a den of thieves!" (Matthew 21:12-13, NLT)

What is prayer? I have often heard statements like this, "I could never sit and talk to God for an hour . . . I run out of things to say after a few minutes!" This type of statement reflects a poor understanding of prayer. Yes, prayer incorporates talking *to* God, but it is much more.

Prayer is communication and communion with God. Good communication requires listening as well as speaking. Communion is a depth of intimacy. Prayer is being with God and practicing being in His presence. In 1 Thessalonians 5:17, the Apostle Paul tells us to pray continually. The impossibility of sitting with your eyes closed and hands folded makes Paul's encouragement seem ridiculous to those who may not grasp the true concept of prayer.

Every relationship incorporates a variety of interactions and communications. Sometimes just being in the presence of your best friend, spouse, parent, or sibling is all that is needed. Some call this shoulder-shoulder time, like going for a walk or driving in a car. But there are times we need to have intimate and transparent conversations. The same is true of our relationship with God. Prayer can be an intimate and transparent conversation, but it can also be practicing awareness of God's indwelling presence.

As the temple of the Holy Spirit, we are continually in His presence. This means He can speak to us when we need guidance. Jesus said His Holy Spirit will "guide you into all the truth" (John 16:13). This means the Holy Spirit will bring Scripture to our recollection when we need it, give us the words to say when He leads us to speak to someone, and bring to our attention things God places in front of us to accomplish. The Holy Spirit also convicts us of sin with a godly sorrow that will lead us to repentance so that our relationship with Him will not be hampered. All of this can take place in intimate prayer times or in shoulder-shoulder time. Because God has made His dwelling in you, you can live in a continual attitude of prayer!

> As the temple of the Holy Spirit, we are continually in His presence.

The Temple is a Place of Worship

Jesus replied, "Believe me, dear woman, the time is coming when it will no longer matter whether you worship the Father on this mountain or in Jerusalem. You Samaritans know very little about the one you worship, while we Jews know all about him, for salvation comes through the Jews. But the time is coming—indeed it's here now—when true worshipers will worship the Father in spirit and in truth. The Father is looking for those who will worship him that way. For God is Spirit, so those who worship him must worship in spirit and in truth." (John 4:21-24, NLT)

"I appeal to you therefore, brothers, by the mercies of God, to present your bodies as a

living sacrifice, holy and acceptable to God, which is your spiritual worship." (Romans 12:1)

I began full-time pastoral ministry as a worship pastor. This title is commonly used in churches all over the world, including the one where I serve as lead pastor. However, the title is a bit misleading. When using the title *worship pastor*, churches literally refer to individuals who leads the congregation in singing worship songs. Worship is biblical; I love worshiping through music, and God loves being worshiped through music. Worship, though, incorporates more than singing and playing instruments. By bringing glory to God and proclaiming the goodness of God, we worship. We can worship in the attitude of our hearts, the words of our mouths, and the work of our hands. As Paul reminds us, "Whether you eat or drink, or whatever you do, do it all for the glory of God" (1 Corinthians 10:31, NLT).

When Jesus taught His disciples to pray, He began His prayer, commonly known as The Lord's Prayer (Matthew 6:9-13), by proclaiming God's holiness—a statement of worship. Jesus demonstrated that worship, then, is an important part of prayer. You are the temple of God. You are a house of worship. In song, in prayer, and literally in all you do, you can bring glory to God!

Read once again what God promised at the dedication of Solomon's temple:

My eyes will be open and my ears attentive to every prayer made in this place. For I have chosen this Temple and set it apart to be holy— a place where my name will be honored forever. I will always watch over it, for it is dear to my heart. (2 Chronicles 7: 15-16, NLT)

This promise of committed attentiveness extends to you as well. You are a dedicated and set apart temple of the Holy Spirit where God desires to dwell. You are a 24/7 house of prayer and worship, and you . . . yes, *YOU*, are dear to God's heart. This is yet another way in which God took the initiative and demonstrated that He...

Loves Us First!

Reflect . . .

1. What are some of the characteristics of Solomon's temple?

2. What did God say about His temple?

3. What does it mean for you to be a temple of the Holy Spirit?

4. What does it mean for us to be holy? How are we made holy? When does that happen?

Chapter 8
You Belong

So now you Gentiles are no longer strangers and foreigners. You are citizens along with all of God's holy people. You are members of God's family.

Ephesians 2:19 (NLT)

I arrived on the university campus the afternoon prior to my first day of class. As my supervising professor gave me a quick tour, I was overwhelmed with feelings of excitement and just a touch of anxiety. I had dreamed of pursuing a Ph.D. for years, and now that dream was beginning to be realized. After completing the final paperwork for registration and accommodations, I headed straight for the University of Buckingham bookstore. I needed a couple of books, but most importantly, I needed school paraphernalia. I bought a University of Buckingham pen, sweatshirt, cap, and scarf. After all, that's what you are supposed to do. I was not only officially a student, but I looked like one, too!

> We all need to know we belong.

It seems everywhere I look, I see bumper stickers, t-shirts, and other indicators of favorite teams, schools, universities, and groups with whom individuals choose to identify. We all need to know we belong. By our shirts and bumper-stickers, we are telling the world, "I belong! I am a part of a tribe!" This innate longing to belong is natural.

One of our greatest fears is being alone. We were never meant to be alone. We are social creatures. I understand some people desire to live in solitude, but the great majority of us long to be a part of something bigger than ourselves. In fact, in many ways, we get a sense of our identity by the context of our relationships. We will address relationships more intimately in part three, but first, it is important to understand how God's love impacts our sense of identity. If our relationships define us, then our principal, defining relationship is the one with God. We have already looked at how we are the children of God and the temple of the Holy Spirit. These and the following positions we hold with God greatly inform our identity.

You are IN Christ!

Christians often inquire of others, "Have you asked Jesus into your heart?" This question is asking whether a person has surrendered their life to Jesus, accepted His sacrifice on the Cross as payment for their sin, and invited His Holy Spirit to fill them. When someone becomes a follower of Jesus, His Spirit comes and dwells in them. That's why Christians ask, "Is Jesus *in* your heart?"

This description is an accurate portrayal of the relationship between a believer and Christ, and yet despite this commonly phrased question, eighty-eight times in the New Testament we read that believers are "in Christ!" Here are just a few examples:

> *And because of him you are **in Christ** Jesus, who became to us wisdom from God, righteousness and sanctification and redemption.* (1 Corinthians 1:30)

> *Therefore, if anyone is **in Christ**, he is a new creation. The old has passed away; behold, the new has come.* (2 Corinthians 5:17)

> *There is therefore now no condemnation for those who are **in Christ** Jesus.* (Romans 8:1)

In other words, when someone becomes a Christ-follower, not only does Christ live in them through His Holy Spirit, they become *in relationship* with Christ.

This relationship is clearly seen in the important tradition of baptism. In baptism, believers publicly professes their faith in Jesus and symbolically identify with Him in His death (by declaring their old self to be dead), burial (by being literally immersed in water), and resurrection (by rising out of the water ready to walk in a new life in Christ). Baptism is a picture of being immersed into a relationship with Jesus. We are baptized into the body, or family, of Jesus!

You are a Citizen in God's Kingdom!

If you are *in* Christ, you are no longer *of* the world even though you are *in* the world. The Apostle Paul writes, "To the saints and faithful brothers *in* Christ *at* Colossae" (Colossians 1:2). *In* Christ is not a place but a system, a citizenship, a relationship! I was born in the United States, and I am a United States citizen. On occasion I have the opportunity to travel outside of the United States. While I am in another country, I am still a U.S. citizen. My present location does not supersede my citizenship. Jesus said, "You do not belong to the world, but I have chosen you out of the world" (John 15:19).

> *In* Christ is not a place but a system, a citizenship, a relationship!

Certain responsibilities accompany citizenship of any nation. As a citizen of God's Kingdom, there are also expectations and responsibilities we are to accept. Sometimes these responsibilities and expectations are viewed as rules or legalism. Unfortunately, there are those who approach God's expectations of us as rigid rules; however, God's expectations have purpose and are intended to help us to become like Him and to live an abundant and fulfilled life (discussed in more detail in the next section).

As a Christian, you no longer belong to the world because you belong to God:

So now you Gentiles are no longer strangers and foreigners. You are citizens along with all of God's holy people. You are members of God's family. (Ephesians 2:19, NLT)

You are a Member of God's Family!

Psalm 68:6 says, "God sets the lonely in families." Human longing to belong mirrors our longing for God. This innate longing that drives us to be connected to others is demonstrated throughout our school years.

Society sees young people drawn to groups or cliques because of the need to belong. In order to gain acceptance, they begin dressing, talking, and acting like the other members of their clique. Those who don't fit in with any clique are recognized as outsiders or loners. While young people will often go to great extremes to fit into a group, this behavior is not exclusive to the young but is seen throughout adult lives as well. We all long to be connected to a family, and God's family is a global network of brothers and sisters. We may have different languages and customs, and even some doctrinal differences, but we are family.

I have a vivid memory of that comforting sense of family from when I was at the University of Buckingham. After a long and exhausting day of class, I walked out of the building with a couple of my colleagues. I was missing my family, and I was feeling a little lonely. As we walked down the stairs, I glanced through a window at a group of people gathered in a circle with a portable stereo on the table near them. Their eyes were closed, their hands were raised, and they were singing. Within seconds I recognized them as family.

> We all long to be connected to a family, and God's family is a global network of brothers and sisters.

Although this was not a religious university, and although I was in England, thousands of miles from home, I felt a warm reminder that I was not alone. I was connected to this group of people. They were my family. I never met any of those students. I don't know their names, and I don't know from what countries they came, but I do know they are my brothers and sisters.

You are a Member of the Body of Christ!

Just as a body, though one, has many parts, but all its many parts form one body, so it is with Christ. For we were all baptized by one Spirit so as to form one body—whether Jews or Gentiles, slave or free—and we were all given the one Spirit to drink. Even so the body is not made up of one part but of many. Now if the foot should say, "Because I am not a hand, I do not belong to the body," it would not for that reason stop being part of the body. And if the ear should say, "Because I am not an eye, I do not belong to the body," it would not for that reason stop being part of the body. If the whole body were an eye, where would the sense of hearing be? If the whole body were an ear, where would the sense of smell be? But in fact God has placed the parts in the body, every one of them, just as he wanted them to be.

If they were all one part, where would the body be? As it is, there are many parts, but one body. The eye cannot say to the hand, "I don't need you!" And the head cannot say to the feet, "I don't need you!" On the contrary, those parts of the body that seem to be weaker are indispensable, and the parts that we think are less honorable we treat with special honor. And the parts that are unpresentable are treated with special modesty, while our presentable parts need no special treatment.

But God has put the body together, giving greater honor to the parts that lacked it, so that there should be no division in the body, but that its parts should have equal concern for each other. If one part suffers, every part suffers with it; if one part is honored, every part rejoices with it. Now you are the body of Christ, and each one of you is a part of it. (1 Corinthians 12:12-27)

Take a moment and think of all the body parts you are using in order to read this book. As I stopped to consider this, I realized that, in essence, my whole body was working together to perform this very simple task. Without one part, simply reading a book changes significantly. I can't say, "To read, I don't need my lungs or hands." Each body part is important. The Apostle Paul said those parts that seem to be weaker are, in fact, indispensable! Not only did God love you enough to make you a citizen of His Kingdom, adopt you as His child, and make you a member of His family, He also loved you enough to make you an indispensable part of His Body! We are not all the same, but we are all valuable. God knows you need a place to belong. He knows you need a family, but He also knows the family needs you!

God Chose You!

Two team captains stand before a lineup of children waiting to be chosen for a team. "I choose Tommy," announces the first team captain. The other captain chooses Bill. One by one, team members are chosen according to ability or popularity. You are one of three left not chosen. Your neighbor is picked next, and you find yourself pleading under your breath, "Please choose me." None of us wants to be the last one picked for a team. Being chosen last announces to the world and to ourselves that we are not really good enough; we are not really wanted. We have probably all been in some situation in which this question of our worth and desirability has arisen.

Now imagine the God of the universe standing before all of the men and women He has ever created. Each person is feeling insignificant and waiting to hear God say, "I choose *(your name)*." This is a scenario you do not have to imagine, hope, fear, or dream. God has already called you by name! He chose you! Isaiah 43:1 says, "Do not be afraid, for I have ransomed you. I have called you by name; you are mine" (NLT). In John 15:16, Jesus tells His followers, "You did not choose Me, but I chose you." What a powerful encouragement to know that God has handpicked you.

You Belong!

We were created for relationship with God and for relationship with God's family. Everything from how many team t-shirts we have in our wardrobes, what bumper stickers are on our cars, and our Facebook profile pictures, our desire to belong betrays us.

We know deep inside that our affiliation with teams or groups is purely superficial and temporal. We know there must be more. Some fundamental questions of life are, *"Who am I?"* and, *"Where do I belong?"* God answers those questions for us. He has placed us in relationship with himself and with His people.

Your identity is grounded in your relationship with God. You are invited to become a part of God's Kingdom, His family, and His body. You were meant for community, and your relationship with God places you firmly in community from now through eternity. You were never meant to go through life alone.

All of us know how cold it is outside. It's almost unbearable out there. Especially when we're there alone, isolated, lonely. You were never meant to be . . . alone.

(Erwin McManus- Soul Cravings)

Reflect . . .

1. With what teams, universities, church groups, or other tribes do you identify?

2. How do you demonstrate your belonging?

3. Did you choose these tribes or were you chosen? If you chose a particular group or tribe, why did you choose them?

4. What are some of the most meaningful ways in which you relate to God?

5. What are some of the most meaningful ways in which you relate to the people of God?

Part 2
Love First:
Loving God First

Chapter 9
Loving God by Obeying God

"If you love Me, you will keep My commandments."

John 14:15

Obedience. One of those words I don't like. It's like *discipline, confrontation, accountability,* and other words that describe difficult, and often unnatural work. Most of us do not appreciate being told what to do. I am no exception. If asked nicely, I will do just about anything. However, when I feel manipulated or commanded, I strongly resist . . . you might say I even rebel.

Before passing judgment on me, ask yourself, "How do I respond to orders?" If you serve in the military, I suspect you respond well. Obedience to commands is an expectation and allows the military to function efficiently. If you are not serving in the military, you probably respond to commands the same way I do. Our human DNA screams out for autonomy and freedom: "I want my own way!" Human nature simply doesn't like to be told what to do.

> While we may not like the idea of being obedient, we all live in obedience.

While we may not like the idea of being obedient, we all live in obedience. We must ask ourselves, "To whom, or to what, am I obedient?" The great philosopher, Bob Dylan, put it this way:

You're gonna have to serve somebody, yes, you're gonna have to serve somebody. Well, it may be the devil, or it may be the Lord, but you're gonna have to serve somebody.

Jesus said no one can serve two masters; we will love one and hate the other. Our allegiance lies somewhere. And while we may have obedience to another person, many of us live in obedience to our fleshly, human nature. Self, pleasure, money, addictions, material gain, fame, prestige, and the favor of people, to name a few, can all demand our obedience. Romans 8:12 says, "Therefore, dear brothers and sisters, you have no obligation to do what your sinful nature urges you to do" (NLT). We are not obligated to obey those fleshly desires, but we often do.

In the Beginning

The Bible begins with the topic of obedience. Genesis 2:16, shortly after the creation of Adam, is the first command given to humankind by God:

The LORD God commanded the man, saying, "From any tree of the garden you may eat freely; but from the tree of the knowledge of good and evil you shall not eat, for in the day that you eat from it you will surely die."

The Bible then tells us God created Eve because He saw it was not good for man to be alone. Shortly afterward, Satan appeared to tempt Adam and Eve to eat from the forbidden tree. He questioned their obedience and offered what seemed to be a better way than God's way.

When God came to the garden to visit, He noticed Adam and Eve were in hiding. Upon questioning them, Adam said that they were naked and afraid.

Adam and Eve were given one command and they disobeyed. Obedience was the one condition of life in the Garden of Eden. Their disobedience set the course for all humankind. We perpetually struggle with the root of that original sin, "I want to be god . . . at least in my own life!" This has become our human nature: self-centered and self-serving. One of our first words is, "Mine." Our lives naturally revolve around "me."

We spend our lives accumulating, achieving, and living in full submission to our self-centered nature. When we feel unfulfilled, that nature says, "Find fulfillment!" We obey without thinking twice. But each time we obey, we still feel empty. Nothing seems to satisfy our longing, so we keep obeying its incessant commands.

In the Middle

In the middle of the story of humankind and
God, obedience continued to play a vital role.
Abraham was commanded to leave his home
country, and he was commanded to offer his son,
Isaac, as a sacrifice to God on an altar. Moses was
commanded to lead God's people out of Egypt. On
one occasion, during forty years of wondering
around the wilderness, the people became thirsty
because there was no water. God said to Moses:

> *"You and Aaron must take the staff and
> assemble the entire community. As the people
> watch, speak to the rock over there, and it will
> pour out its water. You will provide enough
> water from the rock to satisfy the whole
> community and their livestock."*

> *So Moses did as he was told. He took the staff
> from the place where it was kept before the
> Lord. Then he and Aaron summoned the people
> to come and gather at the rock. "Listen, you
> rebels!" he shouted. "Must we bring you water
> from this rock?" Then Moses raised his hand
> and struck the rock twice with the staff, and
> water gushed out. So the entire community and
> their livestock drank their fill.*

> *But the Lord said to Moses and Aaron,
> "Because you did not trust me enough to
> demonstrate my holiness to the people of Israel,*

you will not lead them into the land I am giving them!" (Numbers 20:8-12, NLT)

I must admit it is easy to sit in the comfort of my air-conditioned home, with cooled and purified water readily dispensable from my refrigerator and criticize the people of Israel for their grumbling. I have been to that desolate wilderness and, even in February, it is hot, dusty, and formidable. I confess, I would probably have been the first to say, "Why did you bring us out here to die of thirst? We should have stayed in Egypt where we at least had water, food, and shelter!"

Being a leader is difficult. Moses had become frustrated with the grumbling people, and he was thirsty, hot, and tired just as they were. In an act that doesn't seem too evil, he struck the rock with his staff rather than obediently speaking to it. Water flowed freely, yet Moses had not acted in obedience. His disobedience in this seemingly small matter was enough to keep him from entering the Promised Land. Severe punishment? Yes, but it is a testament to the value God places on obedience.

In the End

The last book of the Bible refers, again, to the importance of obedience. In Revelation 22:7, Jesus speaks to the Apostle John, "Behold, I am coming soon! Blessed is he who keeps the words of the prophecy in this book." Keeping, or obeying, the words of the prophecy of the Bible is a means to God's blessing.

God always rewards our obedience, and He always disciplines our disobedience. His discipline may seem harsh at times, as with Moses; however, we must remember God's discipline is for training us. His discipline is not punitive but restorative in nature.

> God always rewards our obedience, and He always disciplines our disobedience.

In Genesis and throughout the Bible, we read story after story of God's relationship with His people. When they disobey, they are disciplined. When they obey, they are blessed. If the fruit of obedience is blessing, I will strive to obey!

Why Obey God?

As children, we intuitively ask a crucial question when we are told things, especially when we are told to do something, "But, why?" It is a question parents find annoying and is often answered with a sharp, "Because I said so!" We may find ourselves asking the question, "Why should I obey God?" The answer could be a snappy,

"Because the Bible says so!" And while that is true, is it inspirational enough to truly illicit obedience?

Why should we obey God? One reason is because He blesses obedience and punishes disobedience. As we previously discussed, we find multiple examples in the Bible of God rewarding those who obey Him, and we also find many examples of God disciplining those who do not. Is receiving a blessing from God a good motivator? Sure it is. But I contend it isn't the best source of motivation. Is avoiding punishment or discipline a good motivator? Again, yes, it is, but there is still a better source.

So, what is the best motivation? The Apostle Paul tells us the answer to that secret:

> *But now let me show you a way of life that is best of all. If I could speak all the languages of earth and of angels, but didn't love others, I would only be a noisy gong or a clanging cymbal. Three things will last forever—faith, hope, and love—and the greatest of these is love.* (1 Corinthians 12:31-13:1, 13, NLT)

The entire thirteenth chapter of 1 Corinthians is considered "The Love Chapter." It is often quoted at weddings and is familiar to many who are unfamiliar with anything else the Bible says.

The Apostle John wrote in his first letter that God is love. In the Gospel of John, Jesus says, "Greater love has no one than this, that someone lay down his life for his friends" (John 15:13). The answer to, "Why," is one simple word: *love*.

Because God took the initiative to love us first, it compels us to love Him . . . first. Jesus said, "If you love Me, you will keep My commandments" (John 14:15). When we have grasped God's love for us, we are then able to freely love Him in return. From this point forward, obedience is not motivated by a carrot or a stick but is inspired by love.

The Example of Jesus

Jesus *Showed* Us

Jesus is the greatest example of what it means to live an obedient life for God. Even from childhood, we see Jesus busy doing His Father's business. Once, when Jesus was twelve years old, His parents took Him to the Feast of the Passover in Jerusalem. On the way home, about a day's walk, His parents realized they couldn't find Him. They retraced their steps and found Him back in Jerusalem talking with the teachers. When questioned about why He stayed behind, Jesus said that they should have known He would have been in His Father's house (Luke 2:41-49).

In addition to a dwelling, the word *house* can also mean "affairs or business," as the King James

Version translates it. In either case, Jesus placed priority on being fully invested in the things of His Father, God.

> Obedience was life-giving sustenance to Jesus.

Throughout Jesus' life, we see Him living in complete submission to the Father's will and not His own. In John 4:34-35, Jesus said that His food was to do the will of God the Father. Obedience was life-giving sustenance to Jesus. Jesus relinquished all His desires, all His passions, all His life into the hands of God, and lived life saying, "Not my will, Father, but yours."

Jesus *Told* Us

Jesus not only showed us how to obey, but He also taught us to obey. In Matthew 7:24-27, Jesus says:

Everyone then who hears these words of mine and does them will be like a wise man who built his house on the rock. And the rain fell, and the floods came, and the winds blew and beat on that house, but it did not fall, because it had been founded on the rock. And everyone who hears these words of mine and does not do them will be like a foolish man who built his house on the sand. And the rain fell, and the floods came,

*and the winds blew and beat against that house,
and it fell, and great was the fall of it.*

How can we know the commands of God? By knowing the Bible. Joshua 1:8 declares that God's people should meditate on the Word of God day and night so that we will be able to do everything it says. This is followed by a promise that God will bless us with prosperity and success.

What are some of the commands we find in the Bible? Perhaps the most well-known are the Ten Commandments God gave to Moses (Exodus 20:1-17):

1. You shall have no other Gods before me.

2. You shall not make for yourselves an idol.

3. You shall not misuse the name of the LORD your God.

4. Remember the Sabbath day by keeping it holy.

5. Honor your father and your mother.

6. You shall not murder.

7. You shall not commit adultery.

8. You shall not steal.

9. You shall not give false testimony.

10. You shall not covet.

As others have pointed out before, the first four commands have to do with our relationship with God. The last six commands deal with our relationship with others. This is why Jesus was able to sum up all the commandments into two: love God with all your heart, soul, mind, and strength, and love your neighbor as yourself (Matthew 22:34-40). In other words, we are to love first.

Throughout the Scriptures, we find numerous commandments which can be summed up in Jesus' statement. If we love God, He will be our first love and the one we place first in our lives. We will strive to become like Jesus and live lives pleasing to Him. If we love God, we will obey His commands.

> If we love God, we will obey His commands.

The Apostle Paul, through the inspiration of the Holy Spirit, wrote multiple times that we are to place others above ourselves. We demonstrate our love for God in the way we love people. Love for others will necessarily include our concern for their souls.

The purest demonstration of loving God by obeying His commands and loving others culminates in Matthew 28:19-20:

Therefore, go and make disciples of all nations, baptizing them in the name of the Father and of the Son and of the Holy Spirit, and teaching them to obey everything I have commanded you. And surely, I am with you always, to the very end of the age.

Loving God first, is seen in our obedience to His command to love others.

Reflect . . .

1. Do you like to be told what to do? How do you typically respond to a command from another person?

2. How does that internal response impact the way you respond when you are given a command by God, either in His Word or through the Holy Spirit?

3. Can you think of a time you disobeyed God? What happened?

4. What are some examples of Jesus being obedient to the Father? What are other examples in the Bible of people who either obeyed or disobeyed God?

5. Why should we obey God?

Chapter 10
Thine, Not Mine

*"Father, if you are willing, remove this cup
from me. Nevertheless, not my will, but yours,
be done."*

Luke 22:41-42

The Kidron Valley of Jerusalem felt like an
oven. As I made my way from the Upper Room to
the Garden of Gethsemane, I contemplated what
Jesus must have been going through as He walked
this path with His disciples on the night of His
betrayal.

Having just finished eating together and after
releasing Judas to go and take care of his business,
the band of companions were probably pretty quiet
and somber. Perhaps they talked quietly among
themselves. "What is going on? This is certainly not
a typical Passover meal . . . and what is up with
Judas? He was sure acting strange!"

Jerusalem, in the middle of July, is often
sweltering, and this day was exceptionally hot. As
sweat dripped from my forehead, I thought, "Is this
worth it?" I wondered if Jesus may have had a
similar question as He walked the same path. As He
reached the Garden and began praying, we are told

that drops of blood dripped from His forehead. Perhaps He asked, "Are *they* worth it?"

As He continued in prayer, He said, "Father, if You are willing, remove this cup from Me; yet not My will, but Yours be done" (Luke 22:42). His entire life had been consecrated for this moment, yet He prayed the Father would take it away. My discomfort was certainly no comparison to what Jesus was internally experiencing. Knowing He was about to be crucified for the very same people who would first mock, reject, and beat Him had to have been almost unbearable. Unbearable, but He was willing and obedient.

> Jesus has set for us an example of extreme obedience.

Jesus has set for us an example of extreme obedience. Although obedience to the Father's will at the time seemed intolerable, He endured because the end of the story has more eternal significance than the middle of the story. Jesus' example of how He navigated that night in the Garden of Gethsemane is encouraging.

Jesus prayed in the Garden for God's will to be done. He was able to pray this because of His trust in God the Father. We also can trust that God, our

Father, has our best interest at heart and that He can make our lives more significant than we can.

We all want to make a positive impact with our lives. And Jesus taught us that to have that impact, we should pray for God's will to be done: "Pray, then, in this way: 'Our Father who is in heaven, Hallowed be Your name. Your kingdom come. Your will be done'" (Matthew 6:9-13). Jesus *told* us and He *showed* us to pray for and to obey God's will.

Building on the example of Christ, James also taught that we should strive to live in God's will:

> *Come now, you who say, "Today or tomorrow we will go to such and such a city, and spend a year there and engage in business and make a profit." Yet you do not know what your life will be like tomorrow. You are just a vapor that appears for a little while and then vanishes away. Instead, you ought to say, "If the Lord wills, we will live and also do this or that."* (James 4:13-15)

We do not know what the future holds. Most of us have experienced, at least once in our lives, a moment in time—a word, a choice, an action—that completely changes the direction we are heading. So, James reminds us that we should not be dependent on our plans but instead focus on seeking and obeying the direction of God.

And God does have a specific direction for each of our lives. God spoke through the prophet Jeremiah, "'For I know the plans I have for you,' declares the LORD, 'plans to prosper you and not to harm you, plans to give you hope and a future'" (29:11). Such courage these words should give us all to obey, even in the difficult and unbearable times.

Understanding God's will for our lives is a process and includes several components. When we examine Jesus' prayer in the Garden, we find three distinct elements: wrestling with *me*, resisting Satan, and submitting to God.

Wrestling with Me

Sometimes we forget the Son of God is also the Son of Man . . . literally a human man with all the physical features and capacity for pain as any other human. Jesus knew He must deny himself to fulfil the will of God. His struggle in the Garden was severe. Jesus was fully aware of the enormous responsibility on His shoulders and the great agony He was about to experience.

> Jesus knew He must deny himself to fulfil the will of God.

Some people can get hung up on whether Luke was using a simile or was writing a fact that Jesus sweated blood. This is an argument better suited for the medical and theological experts. *Hematidrosis* is, in fact, a rare medical condition. This condition results when the tiny blood vessels in the skin break and blood flows from the sweat glands. Leonardo DaVinci, for example, wrote about a soldier who sweat blood on the battlefield. The point of Luke's description is that the pressure Jesus was going through, prior to His betrayal, was immense.

I, however, don't believe it was simply the physical trial Jesus was about to endure that weighed the heaviest upon Him that night. Remember, He is the Son of God. He is the third person of the Trinity. Jesus knew no sin. "[God] made Him who knew no sin *to be* sin on our behalf, so that we might become the righteousness of God in Him" (2 Corinthians 5:21).

Consider all the sins you have ever committed. Now add to that list all the sins you will commit before you die. Add to that all the sins of every person you know. Now add the sins of every person living in the world. Now add the sins of every person who has lived up until this day. And finally, on top of all those sins, add the sins of everyone who will ever live. That is a lot of sin . . . a lot of EVIL.

This God-man was about to take upon himself all the sin of all the world. Not only was He going to take that sin upon himself, but His Father was also about to forsake Him.

All this weight was crushing against Jesus as He prayed in the Garden of Gethsemane that night. In fact, the name *Gethsemane* literally means "olive press." It is no wonder Jesus prayed that the Father would take this cup from Him. However, He completed His prayer by committing himself to obey the will of the Father, regardless of the answer.

The Father did not remove that cup and Jesus endured the shame of the Cross. How was He able to make it through that darkest moment of all history? Friedrich Nietzsche is attributed with a powerful statement which, when translated from its original German, says something like this: "He who has a reason *why* can overcome almost any *how*."

This truth is validated in the book of Hebrews concerning the *why* of Jesus' ability to endure the Cross.

"...looking to Jesus, the founder and perfecter of our faith, who for the joy that was set before him endured the cross, despising the shame, and is seated at the right hand of the throne of God."
(Hebrews 12:2)

> He endured because He
> knew the outcome was an
> eternal relationship with you.

We are told that it was for the joy set before Him. The Greek word, *kataphroneó,* translated as "despising the shame" means to count with little regard, or to look past the present circumstance to the result. Remember this: *you* were the joy set before Jesus that night in the Garden and throughout those following hours of agony. He endured because He knew the outcome was an eternal relationship with you.

Jesus was wrestling with the need to deny self and surrender to the will of the Father. Yet He ultimately submitted himself to the Father's will: "Nevertheless, thine, not mine." We face that same struggle today. It is not easy to deny ourselves! How often do we find ourselves making excuses, offering up alternate plans, or just saying, "No"? We plead, beg, and insist that our plan is better than God's. Let's follow the example of Jesus and pray: "Thine, not mine."

Resisting Satan

Jesus began His earthly ministry by being tempted by Satan in the wilderness. There, He was tempted with things that appealed to the flesh or human nature. In the Garden, near the end of His Earthly ministry, Jesus was tempted again, this time to have the terrible cup that was before Him taken away. This was the Devil's last chance to ruin God's plan for redemption. If Satan could just get Jesus to put God's plan off, to find one excuse, or to even say, "no," the Devil would have won!

The Bible does not definitively state whether Jesus was tempted by Satan in the Garden. Hebrews 4:15 does tell us Jesus was tempted during His life in all ways, just as we are, yet was without sin. Mel Gibson's 2004 film, *The Passion of the Christ*, begins with Jesus in the Garden of Gethsemane. Satan comes to Jesus to tempt Him: "No one man can carry this burden, I tell you. It is far too heavy. Saving their souls is too costly. No one. Ever. No. Never." Satan is the enemy of God and God's people. His job description is to steal, kill, and destroy (John 10:10). As Jesus demonstrated in His life, we must resist Satan.

> It is not a question of *if* we will be tempted, it is a question of *when* and *how often.*

How do you resist Satan? First, be alert! 1 Peter 5:8 says, "Stay alert! Watch out for your great enemy, the devil. He prowls around like a roaring lion, looking for someone to devour" (NLT). It is not a question of *if* we will be tempted, it is a question of *when* and *how often*.

Next, pray. In the Garden of Gethsemane, Jesus told His disciples, twice, to pray that they wouldn't fall into temptation. Prayer is so simple, so basic, that it is often relegated to an afterthought. Prayer is, however, one of the most powerful acts in which a follower of Jesus can engage. It is in prayer that we submit to God's authority and invite God's provision. It is in prayer where we communicate with the One who spoke the universe into being and breathed life into our bodies. It is in prayer where, as many Jewish Rabbis have said, heaven and earth kiss.

Third, fight back! The Bible, the Word of God, is listed in Ephesians chapter six as our only offensive weapon—the Sword of the Spirit. We must know the Word. Matthew 4:3-4 says,

> *And the tempter came and said to him, "If you are the Son of God, command these stones to become loaves of bread."*

> *But he answered, "It is written, 'Man shall not live by bread alone, but by every word that comes from the mouth of God.'"*

Satan is the Father of Lies; we must able to speak the truth of the Word to stop Him.

Fourth, we must submit to God. James 4:7 says, "Submit yourselves therefore to God. Resist the devil, and he will flee from you." Submitting is recognizing we may have a certain desire but humbling ourselves to be obedient to God's desire.

Fifth, look again at James 4:7: "Submit yourselves therefore to God. *Resist the devil, and he will flee from you*" (emphasis mine). We must resist! Human beings are often stubborn, and sometimes our stubbornness can be a negative attribute. However, resisting the enemy is simply being stubborn and not giving in. When we submit to God and resist the Devil, the Bible clearly says that Satan will flee!

Submitting to God

Regardless of the pain and agony Jesus knew was before Him, He was committed to obedience. He knew He had to wrestle with His human nature and that He had to resist the temptation of Satan. He could only trust in God's will for His life. This trust in God and subsequent obedience is what we refer to as *submission*. Throughout Jesus' life He *told* us, He *showed* us. He taught us, and He demonstrated for us what it means to submit to the Father.

> Throughout Jesus' life He *told* us, He *showed* us.

When Jesus taught us to seek first the Kingdom of God (Matthew 6:33), He was teaching us to willingly submit to the King. A kingdom must have a territory, subjects, and a king. The territory of God is anywhere His children place their feet. If you are a Christian, you are God's child and ambassador, and you carry with you the kingdom of your Father.

> The territory of God is anywhere His children place their feet.

A kingdom must have subjects. As Christ-followers, we submit to the authority of our King. As King, God then assumes all responsibility for our care and well-being. When we seek to live in His Kingdom, under His rule and authority, we know we are cared for by the God of the Universe. Whatever momentary trial is before us can be endured, like Jesus did, because of the joy that is set before us and awaits us . . . the eternal fellowship we will have with God in Heaven and the reward of hearing the words, "Well done, good and faithful servant!"

As we have observed, in the last days of His Earthly life, Jesus showed us what it means to be obedient to the will of the Father. Jesus prayed, "Father, if You are willing, remove this cup from Me; yet not My will, but Yours be done" (Luke

22:42). His Father did not take away the cup from Jesus, but He did give Jesus the strength necessary to go all the way to the Cross of Calvary. Luke 22:43 says, "An angel from heaven appeared to him and strengthened him." Even when the road of God's will is hard, rely on the strength God will give you to make it. If He has called you to do something, He will provide what you need to obey.

> Obedience to the will of the Father is a choice we must make—and make daily.

Obedience to the will of the Father is a choice we must make—and make daily. Will you pray, along with Jesus, "Thine, not mine"? Can you trust that, although the journey may be difficult, in the end, the reward will be great?

I am reminded of an old gospel song written by Esther Kerr Rushtoi in 1941. The chorus says:

It will be worth it all
when we see Jesus,
Life's trials will seem so small
when we see Christ;
One glimpse of His dear face
all sorrow will erase,
So bravely run the race
till we see Christ.

Reflect . . .

1. Have you ever prayed a prayer similar to the one Jesus prayed in the Garden of Gethsemane: "Father, if You are willing, remove this cup from Me; yet not My will, but Yours be done"?

2. What are some ways you have wrestled with your fleshly/ selfish nature in the past?

3. How have you resisted the temptation of Satan?

4. What does it look like to be in submission to God?

Chapter 11
All of Me

I appeal to you therefore, brothers, by the mercies of God, to present your bodies as a living sacrifice, holy and acceptable to God, which is your spiritual worship. Do not be conformed to this world, but be transformed by the renewal of your mind, that by testing you may discern what is the will of God, what is good and acceptable and perfect.

Romans 12:1-2

In the previous chapter, we looked at Jesus' surrender to the Father's will over His own. As we continue considering how to demonstrate our love for God by our obedience to His will, we now look at how this requires surrendering our minds and bodies. When the Apostle Paul wrote the above passage about presenting one's body to God, it is apparent that he was speaking of our whole being, not just our physical body.

> We not only engage our minds when we submit to the will of God, but we bring our entire being into subjection to Him.

We not only engage our minds when we submit to the will of God, but we bring our entire being into subjection to Him. I grew up singing a children's song called, "Head and Shoulders, Knees and Toes." When I consider obeying God's will, this song reminds me I can surrender all I am to Him.

Head

Since I was a child, I have heard of the importance of having *heart* knowledge and not just *head* knowledge of God. I don't think anyone intended to suggest that we should not engage our brains, but I certainly assumed that the heart takes precedence. Consider the following verses:

> *You keep him in perfect peace whose **mind** is stayed on you, because he trusts in you.* (Isaiah 26:3)

> *"And you shall love the Lord your God with all your heart and with all your soul and with all your **mind** and with all your strength."* (Mark 12:30)

> *For those who live according to the flesh set their **minds** on the things of the flesh, but those who live according to the Spirit set their minds on the things of the Spirit.* (Romans 8:5)

Our minds are as important to God as any other part of our being! He expects us to engage our brains as part of our passionate pursuit of Him! Much of our obedience comes down to a choice to obey. Like Jesus, in the Garden of Gethsemane, when He prayed, "Father, if You are willing, remove this cup from Me; yet not My will, but Yours be done" (Luke 22:42). Jesus made a choice to obey. That choice was made in His mind. That choice is made in our minds. When we contemplate His will for our lives, we must engage our brains! James wrote:

> *Come now, you who say, "Today or tomorrow we will go into such and such a town and spend a year there and trade and make a profit"— yet you do not know what tomorrow will bring. What is your life? For you are a mist that appears for a little time and then vanishes. Instead you ought to say, "If the Lord wills, we will live and do this or that." As it is, you boast in your arrogance. All such boasting is evil. So whoever knows the right thing to do and fails to do it, for him it is sin."* (James 4:13-17)

Some say this passage tells us we shouldn't plan, but that is not what James is saying. James is emphasizing the point that our plans should be made subject to God's will.

Throughout my life I have made plans and set goals. Some of those goals have been achieved and others have morphed into new purposes. One example comes from a point in my life when I was about to complete a master's degree in counseling. I had been serving as an associate pastor in a church, and I was sensing that the time was coming to make a change.

My desire was to do God's will, but without clear direction from Him, I had decided to go into practice with one of my professors. That was *my* plan. A couple weeks prior to graduation, a friend of mine asked what I was going to do upon completion of my degree. I played my cards close to the chest and said I wasn't really sure. He then said that a particular church in town was in search of a lead pastor. I had never wanted to be a lead pastor, so I let out a light chuckle and changed the subject.

That night I could not sleep. I tossed and turned as I began to envision what I might do as lead pastor of that church. A vision and a dream were born. I distinctly felt God's leading to serve as the lead pastor of that church.

The next day, I mentioned this to my boss, the lead pastor for whom I was working. His response was that I should pursue what I sensed was God's leading. He graciously said that if it didn't work out, my job would not be compromised. Within one month, I was elected as the lead pastor of this new church. My plans had never included serving in this capacity, but I remained open to God's will, much like James encourages us to say: "If it is the Lord's will, we will live and do this or that" (James 4:15b). I had to put my mind into serving God's will and not my own plans.

> It has been said that when you fail to plan, you plan to fail!

It has been said that when you fail to plan, you plan to fail! Having a plan is not wrong. In fact, planning is important to our success. I have often used the axiom that it is easier to turn a moving car than a stationary one, and it is easier for God to turn a moving life than it is for Him to turn a stationary life. The key is to keep God in the driver's seat and allow Him to have control of the steering wheel.

As Christ-followers, we recognize that we belong to God. Our lives belong to God. Our plans belong to God. Paul tells us we have been bought with a price and we are no longer our own (1 Corinthians 6:20). Make your plans but keep your mind open to what God desires.

Shoulders

Jesus said, "Take my yoke upon you and learn from me, for I am gentle and humble in heart, and you will find rest for your souls. For my yoke is easy and my burden is light" (Matthew 11:29). The yoke of which Jesus is speaking refers to the teachings of a rabbi.

At that time, a student was symbolically yoked to his teacher much as a young ox is yoked to an older, trained ox. The yoke is a large, wooden beam with cut-outs that allow it to sit upon the shoulders of two oxen, forcing them to walk in step with one another. What the older ox does, the younger does. Where the older ox goes, the younger goes. It is a proven form of training, and the Jews likened following a rabbi to being yoked together with him. By walking together, the older one trains and guides the younger one.

Jesus said that His yoke is easy. Summed up, Jesus' teachings are to love God and to love people. Sometimes it doesn't feel like an easy yoke to bear. In reality, these two simple commands are only easy when He pulls most of the weight! His yoke on your shoulders is a sign of submission. The yoke of submission may be carried on your shoulders, but it is birthed in your heart.

> The yoke of submission may be carried on your shoulders, but it is birthed in your heart.

I was once asked, "What do I do with my ambitions, my hopes, my dreams, my desires? Am I wrong for dreaming?" As discussed in the previous section, plans, ambitions, and dreams are not wrong. In fact, when we are walking in step with the Spirit of God, our dreams and ambitions are often placed in our hearts by the Spirit. The Psalmist says, "Delight yourselves in the Lord and he will give you the desires of your heart" (Psalm 37:4). His desires for us become our desires, His dreams become our dreams, and His plans become our plans. That is the yoke of Jesus in practice!

In Genesis 12:1-3 we read:

Now the Lord said to Abram, "Go from your country and your kindred and your father's house to the land that I will show you. And I will make of you a great nation, and I will bless you and make your name great, so that you will be a blessing. I will bless those who bless you, and him who dishonors you I will curse, and in you all the families of the earth shall be blessed."

God's plan is to bless us; in turn, we will be a blessing to Him and to others. Our plans often come into conflict with God's plans when we are solely fixated on our own self-centered benefits.

Knees

The author of the book, *The Kneeling Christian,* said, "We are never so high as when we are on our knees" (Anonymous, 2007). Of course, prayer doesn't have to take place on your knees, but it is a sign of humility and deference to God. In fact, tradition says that the Apostle James had a nickname of, "Camel Knees." Why? Because he was a man of great prayer.

Prayer is vital when we desire to know God's will for our lives. The previously mentioned passage from Genesis 12:1-3 begins with the statement, "The Lord had said to Abram." God speaks to us through the Bible, the Holy Spirit, and occasionally through others. It is often only in prayer that we are quiet and sensitive enough to hear God speak. If God is going to direct us, show us His will for our lives, we need to be in communication with Him!

The Kneeling Christian reiterates this idea of seeking God's will for "The secret of all failure is our failure in secret prayer!" (Anonymous, 2007) What a powerful thought!

> The secret of all failure is our failure in secret prayer!

Jesus himself took the time to teach His followers to pray, saying, "This, then, is how you should pray: 'Our Father in heaven, hallowed be your name, your kingdom come, your will be done on earth as it is in heaven'" (Matthew 6:9-10). At the beginning of this sample prayer, Jesus prayed God's will to be done. Answers start with looking for God's will—not our own.

Remember that prayer is simply a conversation with God. As in any conversation, we speak and we listen. I have found that my prayer time is often one-sided. I tend to do all of the talking. Sitting silently before God and listening for His voice is essential. For those of us who are task-driven, sitting quietly can seem very unproductive. However, I am always astounded by how often God will speak to me when I take the time and make the effort to listen.

Toes

Our toes are vital to being able to walk well. I was once offered a position in a church and was unsure if I should accept. I asked an older pastor for his opinion, and he replied, "Unless you know God is saying to go, stay put." There is truth to that statement, but it isn't absolute. Sometimes we can become lazy and never step out in faith on the adventure to which God may be calling us.

While studying the life of Moses, I created the acronym F.I.R.E.: Floating, Ignition, Resolve, Effect. I use F.I.R.E to assess where I am on my faith-adventure.

This assessment process begins by acknowledging we all experience seasons of *Floating* (F). These are times when we don't feel like we are going anywhere. We feel stuck, forgotten by God, or like we are having a desert experience like Moses did when he fled to the wilderness after killing the Egyptian. We know we are called to more than this, and during this season we can become very discouraged. However, when we acknowledge we are in a Floating season, we can begin to understand it is a season of preparation rather than stagnation.

There was a season in my life when I sensed deep down that God had called me to move into a new position in a different church. The problem was that the church to which I felt called had another plan. What could I do? I could have gone to the leadership and told them that their plan was not God's will and that I was the one God had called to that particular role. Instead, I sat quietly on the sideline. I felt like Moses in the desert. Lost. Forgotten. Hopeless. In retrospect, I see that the desert experience was not wasted time but preparation time. Preparation for me and for the church to which God would call me.

After a few months, I received a phone call from the leadership of the church. The person they had planned on moving into that position did not sense it was God's will for him. They asked if I would consider it.

Picture the igniting of the burning bush in the desert where God gave Moses the command to, "Go." That is *Ignition* (I)! When we hear God finally give us the green light, we may respond in different ways. Moses argued that he was not competent enough to fulfill his calling. Others run the other direction, like Jonah when he was called to Nineveh and ended up in the belly of whale. And some just choose to obey and go!

When God speaks to me through the burning bush and I receive the command to go, my desire is to see that call as Ignition and take-off. Sometimes we may not have a clear picture of what we are preparing for during our season of Floating. However, if we are paying attention and get the Ignition command to go, then we can take a step into the great unknown while relying completely on God's guidance as we go.

You may think you know exactly what you are supposed to do, but sometimes God changes your course. He may ignite you to move in order to test your faith or to get you started moving in a completely new direction.

Once we have accepted the Ignition of the Lord, we need to seek to be *Resolute* (R). Abraham was Resolute in his obedience to God. Once ignited by God to do something, he began walking out his faith adventure committed to completing his God-calling.

Sometime later God tested Abraham. He said to him, "Abraham!"

"Here I am," he replied.

Then God said, "Take your son, your only son, Isaac, whom you love, and go to the region of Moriah. Sacrifice him there as a burnt offering on one of the mountains I will tell you about."

Early the next morning Abraham got up and saddled his donkey. He took with him two of his servants and his son Isaac. When he had cut enough wood for the burnt offering, he set out for the place God had told him about. On the third day Abraham looked up and saw the place in the distance. He said to his servants, "Stay here with the donkey while I and the boy go over there. We will worship and then we will come back to you."

Abraham took the wood for the burnt offering and placed it on his son Isaac, and he himself carried the fire and the knife. As the two of them went on together, Isaac spoke up and said to his father Abraham, "Father?"

"Yes, my son?" Abraham replied.

"The fire and wood are here," Isaac said, "but where is the lamb for the burnt offering?"

Abraham answered, "God himself will provide the lamb for the burnt offering, my son." And the two of them went on together.

When they reached the place God had told him about, Abraham built an altar there and arranged the wood on it. He bound his son Isaac and laid him on the altar, on top of the wood. Then he reached out his hand and took the knife to slay his son. But the angel of the Lord *called out to him from heaven, "Abraham! Abraham!"*

"Here I am," he replied.

"Do not lay a hand on the boy," he said. "Do not do anything to him. Now I know that you fear God, because you have not withheld from me your son, your only son."

Abraham looked up and there in a thicket he saw a ram caught by its horns. He went over and took the ram and sacrificed it as a burnt offering instead of his son. So Abraham called that place The Lord Will Provide. *And to this day it is said, "On the mountain of the* Lord *it will be provided."* (Genesis 22:1-13)

Although Abraham had Ignition and Resolution, he continued to listen for the voice of God for guidance. Don't you think Isaac was glad his daddy didn't get tunnel vision on the task but continued to walk towards the goal while listening to God!

While you are resolutely walking, you must keep your eyes on Jesus and your ears attentive for His voice. As you go, remember the exhortation of the author of Hebrews, "Let us fix our eyes on Jesus, the author and perfecter of our faith" (Hebrews 12:2).

As we resolutely walk in obedience to the call God has placed on our lives, we will begin to see the *Effects* (E.) In his letter to the Galatians, the Apostle Paul talks about the Fruit of the Spirit, and he goes on to talk about reaping what we sow. Effectiveness is the fruit of sowing in obedience to God's call. Sometimes the effects are immediately apparent. At other times the effects may not come until much later.

I have heard many stories of missionaries called to a certain people group, who they obediently and sacrificially served, and yet went for years without seeing any apparent fruit. For some the fruit was not produced in their lifetime. Sometimes the resulting fruit of our obedience is not what we expect.

> Sometimes the resulting fruit of our obedience is not what we expect.

Regardless of when the fruit of our obedience is produced and whether it is as expected or not, we can trust that when we *Float* with the intention of preparation, *Ignite* in obedience when called to move, and walk in *Resolute* obedience, we will reap the *Effects* of a harvest in due time if we endure and do not grow weary. (Galatians 6:9)

So...

**Use your HEAD and plan.
Take Jesus' yoke on your SHOULDERS. Get on your KNEES and pray.
Get on your TOES and go!**

Reflect . . .

1. Can you think of plans you made and pursued but, somewhere along the way, found that God had intervened, cluttered your course, and set you on a new and more rewarding path?

2. What role has prayer played in your life? Is it important to you?

3. Can you think of times when you felt like you were just *Floating*? Looking back, can you see where God *Ignited* and where you were *Resolute* in your obedience? What was the result or *Effect*?

Part 3
Love First:
Loving Others First

Chapter 12
The Three R's

But God demonstrates His own love toward us,
in that while we were still sinners, Christ died
for us.

Romans 5:8, NKJV

Jim regularly attends First Church. Last week his pastor preached about integrity and the sins of lying and deceit. Convicted about lying on his taxes, Jim sat down on Tuesday and wrote the Internal Revenue Service a letter. He said:

"I have been unable to sleep, knowing that I understated my taxable income. I have enclosed a check for $150.

Sincerely, Jim Marten.
P.S. If I still can't sleep, I will send you the rest."

Everyone likes a good joke about the Internal Revenue Service. It is an organization that breeds animosity, and I have never met someone who has had to deal with them who, afterward, said it was a pleasant interaction. A few years ago, I was audited by the Internal Revenue Service (IRS). As pastors, we can claim mileage as a tax deduction if we travel for the church. I kept records the way I was taught. For years I have recorded my mileage this way. The IRS required me to send in my documentation and then sent a letter rejecting my deduction. They offered no explanation. I went through it again, reformatted my documentation, and still it was rejected. After multiple letters and phone calls, I could get no one to explain why my mileage log was rejected. I felt like I was talking with a brick wall! I became more frustrated than I had ever been.

Then this past year, during tax season, I received numerous automated calls and voicemails from the "IRS" stating that I owed taxes and that if I didn't call immediately and pay those taxes, the local authorities would arrest me, and I would be prosecuted. Of course, I knew this was a scam, and I usually let unknown numbers go to voicemail. But receiving these calls from the IRS (even a fake one), after the frustrating interactions I had already experienced, was making me angry. I was waxing my car on my day off and received another one of these calls. I let it go to voicemail.

After listening to the message, I decided to call them back and let them have it! I called the number, but no one answered, so I called again and again and again. Finally, a man answered in broken English. I began by sarcastically stating how sorry I was for my negligence and acting very concerned. I could have won an Oscar. At one point he interrupted, "Sir, sir, why are you harassing me?"

Are you kidding, I thought!

He went on to say, "You and I both know I don't work for the IRS . . . I have had a very hard day."

I was just about to begin my chastisement when I heard a voice in my head say, "Love first."

I decided to engage the man on the other end in a conversation. I asked where he was calling from and he wouldn't tell me, only that he was not calling from the USA.

I then asked his name. He said he usually tells people his name is Morgan, but it is David. He said he had not had a good day because no one has any money. He added, "We don't take their money unless they can give us $1,000."

I chuckled and asked, "David, do you have a family?" He said he has a wife and two children. "I am guessing that jobs are hard to find where you live and that you are trying to take care of your family?"

He said, "Yes, it is very hard here."

I felt a strong urge to tell him about Jesus and His love, then I said I would pray for him and his family. He responded, "No, I wish you wouldn't!"

I asked, "Why?"

He said, "Because I am afraid of the person you're going to pray to . . . He will curse me!"

I told him that I would not pray for God to curse him but to bless him and his family and that God would reveal himself to them in a miraculous way. I then told him Jesus loves him and Jesus gave His life on the Cross so that David and his family could have eternal life. We talked for a few minutes, and I then politely asked him to remove my name from their call list.

Tax collectors, legitimate or not, have historically been loathed, scorned, and even hated. In the Roman Empire in which Jesus lived, tax collectors were often locals who had been hired by the Romans. Tax collectors were despised by everyone, not only for their job but because they were given the privilege to take as much as they wanted for their own gain in addition to the prescribed Roman tax. They were considered thieves and traitors. Luke 5:27-32 tells the story of an encounter Jesus had with a tax collector:

> *After this he went out and saw a tax collector named Levi, sitting at the tax booth. And he said to him, "Follow me." And leaving everything, he rose and followed him.*
>
> *And Levi made him a great feast in his house, and there was a large company of tax collectors and others reclining at table with them. And the Pharisees and their scribes grumbled at his disciples, saying, "Why do you eat and drink with tax collectors and sinners?"*

And Jesus answered them, "Those who are well have no need of a physician, but those who are sick. I have not come to call the righteous but sinners to repentance."

> The compassion Jesus modeled by intentionally engaging with Levi demonstrates a love first moment.

The compassion Jesus modeled by intentionally engaging with Levi demonstrates a love first moment. Before Levi cleaned up his act, Jesus *loved first,* and His love prompted action.

Jesus regularly ventured into questionable environments to rescue a lost sheep. I am thankful Jesus stepped out of His home in Heaven to come to this planet and rescue me. When we fully grasp the depth of love Jesus has for us and how we have been forgiven, we will be better equipped to love others. Jesus was more concerned with others than He was with His own comfort or reputation. People matter to God, and they matter to those of us who love God. We can love others first because God loved us first.

In Psalm 51, King David walks through a heartfelt prayer of repentance. He begins by confessing and repenting of his sin, recognizing God's gracious forgiveness, and asking God to restore him with His Spirit. David then commits to telling others about God's goodness: "Then I will teach transgressors your ways, and sinners will return to you" (Psalm 51:13). When we realize what God has done for us, we naturally want to share that with others. We want others to experience the freedom and forgiveness Jesus brings.

Jesus actually invites us to love others the way He loves us! One way I remind myself to love others first is by following what I call the Three R's. No, I'm not referring to Reading, Writing, and Arithmetic, but Remember, Recognize, and Renew.

> Jesus actually invites us to love others the way He loves us!

The 3 R's

R1: Remember

Would you please read the following statement out loud?

Remember: Jesus loves me, and He loved me before I was good enough. Before I got cleaned up. Before I put on the right kind of clothes and went to church. Before I started smelling like a Christian. While I was still living in sin, Jesus died for me!

As a child, I never really considered myself a sinner. I have been attending church ever since I can remember. Because of my stepfather's job, we moved often, and every time we moved, we attended the First Baptist Church of every town in which we lived. I was always the good Christian kid. I didn't drink alcohol or do any of the other things a Christian is not supposed to do.

In addition, I did all the things a good Christian *is* supposed to do. I went to church on Sunday mornings, Sunday nights, and to youth group on Wednesday nights. I sang in the youth choir and helped lead in our youth group. I was clean-cut and polite to my elders. I didn't even cuss! I was just like that before I knew Jesus. I grew up, culturally, as a Christian.

However, despite my outwardly Christian appearance, I still needed the sacrifice and resurrection of Jesus to reconcile me with God. I was still an enemy of God. And yet, despite my status as God's enemy, Jesus gave His life for me! The Apostle Paul wrote, in Romans 5:10, that while we were enemies with God, we were made friends with Him through the death and resurrection of Jesus.

Maybe you are a cultural Christian like I used to be. Perhaps you are reading this and you are far from God. You don't look like what you think a Christian should look like. You don't smell like what you think a Christian should smell like. You don't act like what you think a Christian should act like. Jesus loves you. He loves you just as you are. But, He loves you too much to let you stay that way! (I didn't make that up. It's been said by many before me.)

God's love, what the Bible terms His *agape* love, is unconditional and it is undeserved. He loves us regardless of what we do, regardless of what we've done, regardless of how we smell or what our hair is like. He loves us regardless of the color of our skin or how much money we have.

Can you truly grasp the extent of this? God's love is unconditional and undeserved. He loves you—regardless. Many who have been Christians for decades are still not able to fully understand this concept. I am still learning what that means.

Sometimes we are afraid to embrace God's regardless love. We are afraid we will abuse that love and cheapen it. This is a danger. In his book, *The Cost of Discipleship*, Dietrich Bonhoeffer (1995) called this *cheap grace.*

> *Cheap grace is the grace we bestow on ourselves. Cheap grace is the preaching of forgiveness without requiring repentance, baptism without church discipline, Communion without confession . . . Cheap grace is grace without discipleship, grace without the cross,*

*grace without Jesus Christ, living and
incarnate.*

I agree with Bonhoeffer. There are preachers who
preach cheap grace. A genuine relationship with
God is accompanied by an internal transformation
that is demonstrated outwardly. However, we can
remember and embrace God's grace and
unconditional love for exactly what it is:
undeserved and unearned.

A genuine understanding of this love will
inspire us to love Him in return. It will inspire us to
love others in return. However, a partial
understanding of God's unconditional and
undeserved love potentially leads to abusing that
love. I have had people say to me, "It doesn't matter
that I continue to sin, God loves me, and God
forgives me." This is an incomplete understanding
of God's love. It is a danger. But God still takes that
risk on you and on me.

> Genuine love is
> always at risk of being
> abused.

Genuine love is always at risk of being abused.
Genuine love is given without an expectation of
love being returned. Jesus said:

If you love those who love you, what benefit is that to you? For even sinners love those who love them. And if you do good to those who do good to you, what benefit is that to you? For even sinners do the same. And if you lend to those from whom you expect to receive, what credit is that to you? Even sinners lend to sinners, to get back the same amount. But love your enemies, and do good, and lend, expecting nothing in return, and your reward will be great, and you will be sons of the Most High, for he is kind to the ungrateful and the evil. Be merciful, even as your Father is merciful. (Luke 6:32-36)

This is how Jesus loves. Jesus gave His entire life for you and for me as well as for those who mocked Him and crucified Him. "But God demonstrates His own love toward us, in that while we were still sinners, Christ died for us" (Romans 5:8, NKJV). Those who lived in Jesus' time did not deserve His sacrifice, and you and I do not deserve His sacrifice, but regardless of our merit, He loved us with all He had. So, *Remember*:

Jesus loves me and he loved me before I was good enough. Before I got cleaned up. Before I put on the right kind of clothes and went to church. Before I started smelling like a Christian. While I was still living in sin, Jesus died for me!

R2: Recognize

When you observe people, what do you see? It can be difficult for us to separate people from their behaviors. This is partly because we have an innate understanding that what is inside a person spills out. When Jesus looks at people who are far from Him, what does He see? He sees a lost sheep. He sees a person who was created in the image of God but whose image is now shattered.

Do you think Jesus expects a person who does not know Him to live like a person who does know Him? He was not surprised by the lifestyle of Levi, the tax collector. Nor was He surprised by the lifestyles of Levi's friends, other tax collectors and sinners, with whom He had dinner. Jesus expects people who do not know Him to live like they don't know Him. Jesus doesn't ask them to start living like Him prior to coming into relationship with them. When you see others, strive to *recognize* them as God-created human beings and not to only see their behaviors.

Although our behaviors flow from within and, therefore, may describe us, they do not define us. Recognizing that others are not defined by their behaviors is more easily practiced when we *remember* that Jesus loved us prior to our coming into relationship with Him. Because God loved us, we can love Him and we can love others (1 John

4:19). We must *remember* His love for us, but we also must *recognize* the difficulty, if not impossibility, of loving others in our own ability.

Loving others is possible when we love them as a result of being filled with the Holy Spirit. The first result, or fruit, of the Holy Spirit living within us is the fruit of love.

> *But the fruit of the Spirit is love, joy, peace, patience, kindness, goodness, faithfulness, gentleness, self-control; against such things there is no law.* (Galatians 5:22-23)

Some scholars read this passage as saying, "The fruit of the Spirit is love." They say the other fruit are facets of love. This may or may not be what Paul was meaning. However, whether love is one of multiple fruit, or love is *the* fruit, it is inarguably the Fruit of the Holy Spirit. The love of which Paul is speaking is not a natural love but a love empowered by God himself. It is the same type of agape love God gives you and me. It is regardless love. It is undeserved and unearned.

> We can love because it is a result of the transformation and empowerment we experience when the Spirit of the Almighty God lives in us!

How can we love others? By allowing the Holy Spirit to fill us and live through us. We can love because it is a result of the transformation and empowerment we experience when the Spirit of the Almighty God lives in us!

So, *recognize* people as God does: each person is someone who was created in the image of God and that image has been shattered. They are lost, broken, and in desperate need of a savior.

R3: Renew

In Revelation 2:4 (NLT), Jesus said to the Church of Ephesus, "But I have this complaint against you. You don't love me or each other as you did at first!" I love how the New Living Translation includes the phrase, "or each other," which so perfectly captures the concept Jesus intended to convey. Most other translations simply say something like, "You have abandoned your first love." While this is more in alignment with a word for word translation, I do not believe it captures the full intent of Jesus' statement.

Similarly, in 1 John 4:19, I am an advocate for interpreting, "We can love because he first loved us," as, "We can *love God and others* because he first loved us." This fits squarely with Mark 22:37-40 where Jesus says we are to love God and our neighbor as we love ourselves.

The final R, of the Three R's, is to *renew* one's love for God and others. Love must be nurtured and practiced. Love must be renewed on a regular basis. How? By continually being *renewed* by the Word of God and the Spirit of God. Our human nature is to float, to go with the flow. The flow of the world is to cool off, to become stagnant, to deteriorate, or to be fueled by lust and passion.

Renewal must happen regularly. To know God is to love God. The more intimately we know Him, the more deeply we love Him. I believe, therefore, the more deeply we know and love God, the more we will love others. "For God so loved the world." How did He love the world? By sending His son to die for us even while we were still sinners. It is logical, then, that we will begin to love others more as we grow more in love with the Father.

God's love for us is an *agape* love— underserved and regardless love. As we renew our love for God, we will be more able to love others regardless of their actions and attitudes. Someone once argued with me, "If you don't like someone, you certainly can't love them." I disagree. Loving a person does not necessarily mean you will like them. *Like* is based on feelings. If someone treats me or others poorly, I probably will not like them. However, I can still love them. In loving them, I desire for them to come to know Jesus and to accept the gift of life He gives. In loving them, I desire for them to experience the saving grace of God and an abundant life.

> Love is a conscious choice.

Feelings change based on numerous factors. Love is a conscious choice. I can choose to love someone regardless of their actions and regardless of my feelings because Jesus loved me regardless. Reminding myself and intentionally practicing this truth will *renew* my love for others on a regular basis.

When you find it difficult to love someone, pray a simple prayer like this:

Jesus, thank you for loving me when I was not very lovable. Thank you for giving your life for me when I was your enemy. I choose to love [name of person] *with the same kind of love you demonstrated to me. I love them unconditionally, and I love them even when they do not deserve it. I love with your agape love because you first loved me.*

Our love for others flows from our love for God. **If we will take the time to *Remember* that God loved us when we weren't very lovable, *Recognize* others are simply broken and in need of Jesus, just as we are, and *Renew*, or nurture,** our first love for God, then we will be on track to Loving First!

Reflect . . .

1. *Remember*: What were you like prior to knowing Jesus? How does remembering your brokenness help you love others?

2. *Recognize*: How does seeing people the way Jesus sees them help you have grace toward others—even others you don't like very much?

3. *Renew*: What are some ways you can nurture your love for God and for other people?

Chapter 13
When Competition is Loving First

Love one another with brotherly affection.
Outdo one another in showing honor.

Romans 12:10

Have you ever heard the phrase, "The clothes make the man?" Clothes say a lot about a person. Some people are fanatics of sports teams or universities, and they proudly display their loyalties by their clothing. To say my younger brother is a fan of Louisiana State University is a major understatement. I honestly do not think he owns an article of clothing that is not purple and gold. Various sports have their own styles of apparel including biking shorts, tennis outfits, and golf shoes.

Different countries and cultures also have distinct styles of clothing. For some people, clothing can indicate their career, for example, military personnel, medical and dental professionals, firefighters, and police officers. Clothing can also represent different eras. In the 1950-1960's television show, *Leave it to Beaver*, Ward Cleaver, the father, wore a suit and tie to work every day, and when he came home, he got comfortable by exchanging his suit coat for a sweater. June, his wife, would almost always be in the kitchen wearing a dress and heels. Such formal clothing in the home is rarely seen today.

Indeed, over the decades, the clothing style, or dress code, in the United States has overall become progressively more casual. The generally accepted dress code for attending church, including attire for pastors, has also become more casual. Some wear suits and some wear shorts. Overall, today, people tend to just wear what they feel comfortable wearing.

> God's Word always emphasizes the heart over appearance.

While there may be debates among different believers over what is appropriate or not, the Bible clearly addresses what Christ-followers are to wear, but it may not be what you are thinking. The Bible tells us to clothe ourselves with Jesus (Romans 13:14) and to put on the armor of God (Ephesians 6:10-18). In 1 Peter 5:5-6, Peter writes,

> *Likewise, you who are younger, be subject to the elders. Clothe yourselves, all of you, with humility toward one another, for "God opposes the proud but gives grace to the humble." Humble yourselves, therefore, under the mighty*

hand of God so that at the proper time he may exalt you.

God's Word always emphasizes the heart over appearance. When it comes to what to wear, the commands to clothe ourselves with Jesus, the armor of God, and humility are no exception.

Clothe Yourself with Humility

Before we talk about what humility *is*, let's look at what it *is not*. Humility is not weakness, and it is not the same as humiliation. Humility is not continually thinking poorly of oneself nor is it negative, degrading talk. Humility isn't beating oneself up over failures, and it is not a person deflecting when they've done something well.

> Humility is not a quiet, reserved, super sanctimonious posture in life. The truly humble person can be appropriately bold and can enjoy life to the fullest- laughing and crying with great expression. Humility is the driving desire to give God the glory in all things and to obey him regardless. (Stowell, 1996, p. 109)

Is it not our goal that we will hear the Father say to us, "Well done!"?

Some people have a difficult time responding when someone congratulates them on a job well-done. They feel that just simply saying, "Thank you," is prideful. I have wrestled with this myself; I always felt awkward about simply saying, "Thanks!" However, I have learned a humble person can receive commendation without becoming prideful. It has been said that humility is not thinking less of yourself, it's thinking of yourself less. Consider this: If someone thinks they are humble, then they probably are not.

Humility is a Biblical understanding of who you are and how you are called to live. You are a mighty child of God. You are a work in progress. You are someone God works through and works within. You are called to be obedient to God and to serve others. These are biblical facts and not signs of a prideful spirit. Humility is simply loving first. It is placing God first and placing others first. When you love first, you take the first step to clothing yourself as a humble person.

> When you love first, you take the first step to clothing yourself as a humble person.

Getting Dressed

How do you fully get dressed in humility? It's similar to putting on Christ and putting on the armor of God. In fact, getting dressed in humility is like what you did this morning when you got out of bed and put on your clothes. You intentionally picked out what you were going to wear, and then you intentionally got dressed. You put on your pants and your shirt. You put on your socks and your shoes. That's how you clothe yourself with humility: with intentionality.

To get dressed in humility, you have to get up every morning and say, "I'm going to clothe myself with Jesus today. I'm going to put on the full armor of God today. I'm going to clothe myself with humility today." You can intentionally clothe yourself in humility by practicing serving God, serving others, cultivating gratitude, and simply becoming like Jesus.

Practice Makes Perfect

I grew up hearing, "Practice makes perfect," or, "Perfect practice makes perfect," in association with every sport I played. Practice improves muscle memory so we can become more proficient in whatever task we are participating. Playing the guitar, singing, hitting a golf ball, and shooting free-throws all improve with practice. So does humility. Humility becomes habit when we intentionally practice serving God and serving others.

Serving necessarily places us in a humble position toward those we serve. Whether we are serving God, our family, our church, or our neighbor, we are embracing an attitude of humility.

> Serving God flows from recognizing our place in His Kingdom.

Practice Serving God

When we practice serving God, we will become humbler toward God. Serving God flows from recognizing our place in His Kingdom. If He is the King, we are His servants and humbly submit to His rule and authority in our lives. The concept of serving someone is contrary to our current culture. It seems we are constantly hearing of our rights and expressing ourselves in protest every time someone treats us in a way we consider offensive.

The concept of a kingdom is somewhat foreign to most in the world today. Although there are monarchs, like the Queen of England, most are not absolute monarchs. In God's Kingdom, God is the one true monarch. He is the absolute authority. One reason this form of government has been rejected by many people in the world is that absolute power has been demonstrated to corrupt, absolutely. However,

God is all good and wise, and therefore we can completely entrust ourselves to His dominion.

1 Peter 5:6 says, "Humble yourselves, therefore, under the mighty hand of God." This is a command to be obeyed. As with many of God's commands, it is accompanied with a promise. The accompanying promise for humbling ourselves under the mighty hand of God is that He will lift us up.

Think about that phrase, "the mighty hand of God." Sometimes we hear about the mighty hand of God and we think that mighty hand of God is there to bop us on the head every time we mess up. God does discipline those He loves, but His discipline is restorative and not punitive. I think of God's hand as represented in Romans chapter 9:

> *But who are you, O man, to answer back to God? Will what is molded say to its molder, "Why have you made me like this?" Has the potter no right over the clay, to make out of the same lump one vessel for honorable use and another for dishonorable use?" (vv. 20-21)*

God molds us, fashions us for the needs of His Kingdom. His hand is ever shaping us into the clearer image of Christ.

His hand is ever shaping us into the clearer image of Christ.

Yet as Romans 9:20-21 says, we so often look around us and assess ourselves against the purposes for which God has shaped others. Do you ever compare yourself to others and think, "I've worked just as hard as they have," or, "I pray just as much as they do!" "I've done this," and, "I've done that." Notice how often this word, *I,* keeps popping up. The fleshly, self-centered nature within us wants to lift ourselves up and say, "God why are you not blessing me like that?" Humility is being content with who God has made us and content with doing what God has called us to do. We must be faithful with what He's given us to do right here and right now, faithful with who He's made us to be right here and right now.

Be careful of comparison. Comparison is a killer. It will rob you of your joy and it will create envy in your heart. Envy is like a cancer that eats away at you. When you compare yourself to someone else, you either come out better than them or worse than them. Neither one is good for you, and neither one brings glory to God.

God is the potter, and we are the clay, and we can be content with who God has called us to be. When we obediently serve Him and allow Him to guide and direct our paths, we practice humility. Humility is laying aside your self-serving desires to be submissive to what God wants.

God's Kingdom is almost always contrary to the ways of the world. When we want to be truly free, we become His slave; when we want to become first, we become last; and if we want to be lifted up, then we humble ourselves.

> When we live humbly before God, He has the freedom to lift us up.

Jesus told us that if we love Him, we will keep His commandments. If we love Him, we will live a lifestyle that honors Him and is obedient to Him. In Micah 6:8, we read:

He is told, you o' man, what is good; and what does the Lord require of you but to do justice, and to love kindness, and to walk humbly with your God?

When we live humbly before God, He has the freedom to lift us up.

Interestingly, many of God's commands revolve around how we treat others. In serving God, we will necessarily serve other people.

Practice Serving Others

When we practice serving God, we grow in humility. We also grow in humility when we practice serving others. Jesus commanded us to love God and to love our neighbor as ourselves. Loving God and loving our neighbor is demonstrated through service. In the Christian culture, being a servant is generally understood to be a positive attribute. However, not everyone understands why being called a servant is a compliment.

I have a friend who served as the lead nurse on floor in a local hospital. One of her fellow nurses had a reputation for being especially helpful and putting others before herself. On one shift, my friend noticed this nurse going out of her way to serve someone. She said to that nurse, "You are such a servant!" The nurse was deeply offended. For many of us, serving others does not come naturally, and the idea of being a servant requires humility.

As Christ-followers, we have each received spiritual gifts to serve others. Peter writes:

> *Above all, keep loving one another earnestly, since love covers a multitude of sins. Show hospitality to one another without grumbling. As each has received a gift, use it to serve one another, as good stewards of God's varied grace: whoever speaks, as one who speaks oracles of God; whoever serves, as one who serves by the strength that God supplies— in order that in everything God may be glorified through Jesus Christ.* (1 Peter 4:8-11)

The Apostle Paul wrote to the Philippians to consider others as more important than themselves. That is humility.

A humble heart searches for ways to serve others. Romans 12:10 says:

> *Love one another with brotherly affection.*
> ***Outdo*** *one another in showing honor.*

I am a competitive person, and the problem with my competitive nature is if I don't think I can win, I'm not playing. I don't like to play games, but I really don't like to play games I don't know I can win. That's why you will probably never see me playing tennis with my wife. I hate to lose. Competition can be positive, and it can be negative. What Paul describes in the book of Romans is good competition.

We live in a culture where everyone wants to be served and people get offended over every micro-offense. What if every Christian committed to outdo everyone else in showing honor?

> What if every Christian committed to outdo everyone else in showing honor?

I grew up in Texas in a time when, if an older person entered the room, I stood up in honor of that person. I was trained from childhood to say, "Yes, sir," and, "No, sir," and, "Yes, ma'am," and, "No, ma'am." Why? Because such behavior showed honor to my elders. I was taught when someone is walking to the door, you open the door for them. This is etiquette and demonstrates honor. It is an act of humble service.

A couple of years ago, I was driving through the parking lot on my way to a store. I saw an elderly woman pushing a basket loaded with a 50-pound bag of dog food. I thought, "Man, that poor lady is going to have a hard time lifting that into her trunk!" Then I heard the words, "Love first."

I turned down the aisle and put my car in park just behind her car. I jumped out, and I grabbed the bag from her cart. At first, she was startled, thinking someone may be robbing her! When our eyes met, I realized she attends our church. I placed the dog food in her trunk, and she was so thankful. She said, "Oh, Pastor Kent, thank you so much! You're my hero!"

As I got back in my car, I felt very fulfilled and perhaps, just a little bit of pride for being such a selfless and humble servant. Surely, she would tell all of her friends just how much I had blessed her! And then I caught myself. My original intent was not to lift myself up but to love first. This is an example of how we must always be sensitive to our motivation. In practicing serving in humility, we must be careful of our motives. Motive means everything.

A few years ago, I was visiting with an older man in our church. During the conversation, he mentioned that one of our associate pastors went to visit his neighbor in the hospital and how much that meant to his neighbor. I interrupted him mid-sentence and said, "Sorry, it wasn't that associate pastor, it was me." His response still resonates in my heart, "Oh, Kent . . . we've always got to get the glory, don't we?"

> Serving for a reward is really not serving at all.

If we serve with the intent of getting something in return, whether favor or fame, we receive our reward on this earth. Jesus said be careful of practicing your good deeds before others because you'll get your reward right there. Serving for a reward is really not serving at all. It is a transaction. Serving in humility does not require anything in return, including caring who gets the credit.

One good way of testing your motivation in serving others is to ask yourself, "Do I care who gets the credit?" I've got to tell you, it's harder to serve others when nobody sees you serving. My son and I were out snow-blowing this past winter. We went to our next-door neighbor's home and cleared his driveway. He came out and waved.

We, then, went to another neighbor's home, and they didn't come out and wave. They didn't know who cleared their driveway. I thought to myself, "Wow, I wish they would see that it was me . . . maybe I should leave him a note!" If you're truly humbly serving another person, you don't care who gets the credit.

Attention!

Pay close attention to this: Sometimes, serving others requires you to have the humility to let them serve you! For example, a common practice is that when a friend has had surgery or has been ill, people bring them meals. For many of us, accepting help from others is humbling and we typically don't want to be an inconvenience to others.

> Sometimes, serving others requires you to have the humility to let them serve you!

If you don't allow others the opportunity to serve you, you rob them of a blessing. Sometimes demonstrating humility means allowing someone to serve you! When we practice serving others and allow others to serve us, we are practicing a lifestyle of humility.

Cultivate Gratitude

Gratitude promotes humility. Be intentional about recognizing how others have blessed you and quickly say, "Thank you!" I recently read about an African tribe and the way they express gratitude by saying, "I sit on the ground before you." When someone wants to express gratitude, they go and just sit for a period of time in front of the hut of the person to whom they are grateful. It seems a little strange for us, but it's a beautiful picture of humbling oneself and saying, "Thanks for blessing me."

Gratitude promotes humility, and gratitude flows from humility. Consider King David near the end of his life. He first became famous because of a fight with the giant, Goliath. Goliath had a sword, spear, shield and was clothed in armor. David, this young man, approached the giant and said, "You come at me with the sword and the spear, but I come at you in the name of the Lord" (1 Samuel 17:45). David knew if he beat Goliath, it had nothing to do with him and everything to do with who was fighting for him!

Throughout David's life, God gave him victory after victory. But, near the end of his life, we read in 1 Chronicles 21 that Satan rose up against Israel and incited David to take a census. Why would Satan care how many fighting men David had available?

Because Satan wanted David to become prideful. David took the bait, and it didn't end well for him. Satan was cast from heaven because of pride. If he can get us to think victories are our victories rather than God's, if he can get us to become self-reliant, he can take away our effectiveness.

When I became the lead pastor of our church, I said, "I absolutely know that I cannot do this job, and I equally know that through God and in His power, I can do this job." In Him, we can do all things. Apart from Him, we can do nothing.

> Be intentional about recognizing what God has done in your life and be quick to give Him glory.

Be intentional about recognizing what God has done in your life and be quick to give Him glory. That doesn't mean you can't say, "Thank you," when someone says you did a good job, but in your heart, refer that praise right back to God, "God, thank you for using me." Remember to recognize God's hand in your life; cultivate humility by cultivating gratitude.

Become like Jesus

If you want to become humble, then become like Jesus. How do we do that? By knowing God's Word and spending time with Him. Through the Bible, we get to know God's character and His expectations for us. We can read of examples of men and women who lived godly and faith-filled lives. We spend time with God by engaging in prayer and being filled with His Spirit.

Jesus said that He would fill His followers with His Spirit, and in Galatians 5:22-23, Paul tells us about the results or the fruit of the Holy Spirit filling us: "But the fruit of the spirit is love, joy peace, patience, kindness, goodness, faithfulness, gentleness, self-control." Humility isn't listed here because this is not an exhaustive list. Paul is giving examples of what the Fruit of the Spirit in our lives will look like. Humility is a Fruit of the Spirit because it is a characteristic rather of Jesus. Jesus is humble. He is the supreme example of humility, so being filled with His Spirit will promote humility in our lives.

Spending time with Jesus means we need to spend time in His Word and in prayer. Someone once said, "Show me your friends and I'll show you your future." Another truth is you become like the people you hang around with the most. When you spend time with Jesus, you will become like Jesus.

The Apostle John writes of one example of Jesus serving in humility during His last supper with His disciples.

Jesus, knowing that the Father had given all things into his hands, and that he had come from God and was going back to God, rose from supper. He laid aside his outer garments, and taking a towel, tied it around his waist. Then he poured water into a basin and began to wash the disciples' feet and to wipe them with the towel that was wrapped around him. He came to Simon Peter, who said to him, "Lord, do you wash my feet?"

Jesus answered him, "What I am doing you do not understand now, but afterward you will understand."

Peter said to him, "You shall never wash my feet."

Jesus answered him, "If I do not wash you, you have no share with me."

Simon Peter said to him, "Lord, not my feet only but also my hands and my head!"

Jesus said to him, "The one who has bathed does not need to wash, except for his feet, but is completely clean. And you are clean, but not every one of you." For he knew who was to betray him; that was why he said, "Not all of you are clean."

When he had washed their feet and put on his outer garments and resumed his place, he said to them, "Do you understand what I have done to you? You call me Teacher and Lord, and you are right, for so I am. If I then, your Lord and Teacher, have washed your feet, you also ought to wash one another's feet. For I have given you an example, that you also should do just as I have done to you. Truly, truly, I say to you, a servant is not greater than his master, nor is a messenger greater than the one who sent him. If you know these things, blessed are you if you do them." (John 13:3-17)

> Spending time with Jesus means we need to spend time in His Word and in prayer.

Jesus knew how important this teaching and example of humble service would be, not just for His immediate audience but for all His followers from that point forward. However, washing His disciples' feet was only one example of Jesus' humility. The ultimate act of submissiveness and humility before the Father was to be obedient to His will in going to the Cross. Christ's death on the Cross was the ultimate act of humility toward you and to me.

Being found in human form he humbled himself by becoming obedient to the point of death even death on a cross. (Philippians 2:8)

When we practice serving God, practice serving others, cultivate gratitude, and become like Jesus, we will live a life of humility. We will live a life like Jesus . . . a life where we *Love First!*

Reflect . . .

1. Is humility a difficult character trait for you to develop? Why?

2. In what ways does practicing serving God promote humility in our lives?

3. In what ways does practicing serving others promote humility in our lives?

4. How can we learn to cultivate gratitude?

5. What habits do you need to develop in order to become more like Jesus?

Chapter 14
Countering Contempt

Hatred stirs up strife, but love covers all offenses.

Proverbs 10:12

Jeff was arrogant, rude, impatient, and belittling. We worked the late shift together at a rental car company in the airport. It was my first job using a computer, and the company had provided only basic training and then put me to work. Jeff had worked at this company for years. Anytime I asked a question, which admittedly, I had many, he would respond in a condescending and frustrated tone, even when customers were present. Jeff was a bully, and I dreaded going to work. I grew progressively intolerant of his intolerance. I talked with the manager about the potential of not scheduling me with Jeff, but she wouldn't agree. Eventually I decided to resign and work elsewhere.

There are some people I simply do not like. I have trouble liking people who are rude and mean. I have little tolerance for bullies. I am disgusted by men who abuse women and parents who mistreat their children. Of course, violent criminals are on my "Do not like list." There have been times my dislike has even felt like hatred. As a follower of

Jesus, though, I know that hatred is wrong. In fact, I believe most people who don't know Jesus know that hating someone is wrong. But that doesn't stop us. Our present culture seems to condone hate, perhaps even promote it. We hear people talk about acceptance and preach tolerance, but some of those same people will hate an individual if that person disagrees with their perspective.

Our culture has become increasingly divided over the past few years, and in 2020 that divide climaxed. People were intensely divided over the handling of the COVID-19 pandemic. There were those who believed it was all a conspiracy and those who believed it was apocalyptic. There were those who wholeheartedly embraced closing businesses, wearing masks, quarantining, shutting down restaurants, and closing churches. And of course, there were those with the conviction that all of these actions were gross oversteps. I watched as people on social media attacked others because they disagreed with their chosen viewpoint.

In addition to the pandemic, the United States saw riots and protests due to racial tension and the inappropriate behavior of a few police officers. What the pandemic and protests didn't incite, the 2020 elections did. More than a battle of political ideologies, the 2020 elections developed into the hurling of violent accusations against one party toward another. A culture of contempt is alive and thriving in the United States of America.

> A culture of contempt is
> alive and thriving in the
> United States of America.

A Culture of Contempt as the Norm

On February 6, 2020, Harvard University professor and author, Arthur Brooks delivered the keynote address at the National Prayer Breakfast in Washington, D.C. After greeting the distinguished guests, including the President of the United States and others, he began his speech:

> *As you have heard, I am not a priest or minister. I am a social scientist and a university professor. But most importantly, I am a follower of Jesus, who taught each of us to love God and to love each other.*
>
> *I am here today to talk about what I believe is the biggest crisis facing our nation—and many other nations—today. This is the crisis of contempt—the polarization that is tearing our society apart.* (Brooks, 2020, Washington Post)

Brooks is right. This crisis of contempt is ripping our society apart! There is no sin in having strong political and ideological convictions or disapproving of another's behavior, but Jesus clearly compared hatred to murder (Matthew 5:21-22).

When mocked, beaten, accused of blasphemy, and nailed to the cross, Jesus responded to those who hated Him with love and forgiveness. Difficult? Yes. Possible? Yes. But for us, it is only possible by embracing Jesus and allowing Him to transform us from the inside-out. We can love first when others hate us by remembering that Jesus loved first. In a culture where violent contempt has become the norm, Christ-followers can transform.

Jesus Can Transform the Norm

Jesus taught a lifestyle that was counter to His world and ours. In Matthew 5:38-42, Jesus taught that the old philosophy of an eye for an eye should be transformed into one in which we repay evil with good. He taught that we should love our enemies and pray for those who persecute us. This was transformational teaching. Although, really, all of Jesus' teachings were transformational!

Knowing what Jesus taught is easy, but practicing what Jesus taught is often difficult. When I listen to politicians affirming principles which are contrary to biblical standards, I become angry. When I see an innocent person being bullied, I become incensed. Is anger wrong? No. Jesus became angry at the money changers in the temple

(John 2). And the Apostle Paul wrote, in Ephesians 4:26, that when we are angry, we must not sin, and we must not let the sun go down on our anger. So, while there is a place for righteous anger, we must understand that there is a distinction between anger and hatred.

> Anger can easily become bitterness and contempt if not confronted.

Anger can easily become bitterness and contempt if not confronted. Sometimes that confrontation may come from a trusted and concerned friend, but it often comes from the Holy Spirit. He is a Christian's internal guide. If we are sensitive to the Holy Spirit, He will alert us when we sin or are about to sin!

Our desire to become like Jesus drives us to manage our anger before erupting into cancerous contempt. Managing our anger begins with surrender to the Holy Spirit, the Spirit of Jesus. Breathing a simple prayer in the heat of the moment, can deescalate our natural emotional reaction and give us enough time to think through our calculated response.

"Jesus, I surrender this situation to you. You know I am angry but help me to respond in a way that you would respond."

We understand that our anger is not sin, but our reactions may very well be. In submitting our emotions to Jesus, we can begin the process of working through a situation in a manner that honors him. The rest of the process can unfold in a biblical manner, as far as you are concerned, if you will humbly reflect on the situation, remove the log from your own eye (Matthew 7:5), and love first. There is no guarantee the other will respond biblically, but you, as far as you are able, are to live at peace with others. (Romans 12:18)

Love Your Enemies

In teaching us to love our enemies, Jesus proclaimed the cure for contempt. Choosing to love first is a choice. It is a discipline. Loving first is choosing to love when others hate and disciplining our minds to remember how Jesus first loved us. When others spew hatred and contempt, we naturally react, but we can discipline ourselves to react like Jesus . . . to be disciples of Jesus.

The cure for contempt is God, and God is love. As Proverbs 10:12 says, "Hatred stirs up strife, but love covers all offenses." We must discipline ourselves—slow our minds to think through what is being said and what we are saying, pause our tongues (or our typing fingers), and ask God how we can show love in all situations.

> In teaching us to love our enemies, Jesus proclaimed the cure for contempt.

We Can Love First by being Peacemakers

Jesus said peacemakers will be blessed. How do we make peace? There are some people who are uninterested in living in peace with us. We can love them, pray for them, and be kind toward them, but if someone else doesn't want to live in peace with us, there is not much more we can do. However, the Apostle Paul tells us we should do all we can to live in peace with others (Romans 12:18). In other words, we must do what we can and leave the rest up to God.

Striving to live in peace requires humility before God and people. When we are humble before God, we submit to His will and choose to obey His commands. His commands include loving our neighbors as ourselves, even if they are not very lovable—even if they disagree with our political ideology! That kind of love flows from a humble heart.

> Loving first is an attitude of the heart, but it's also physical action.

Real Love Moves

Loving first is an attitude of the heart, but it's also physical action. It is easy to say, "I love you," but love is demonstrated in our actions (1 John 3:18). By making the effort to *do* something kind for another person, even a person with whom we disagree, we can show that person the love of Jesus. **None of us will like everyone, and not everyone will like us. But when we love first, we can become peacemakers and we demonstrate the love of Jesus to the world around us.**

Reflect . . .

1. What "pushes your buttons?" What things cause you to strongly react in anger to people or their behaviors?

2. Do you have bitterness, residual anger, or contempt for someone? Who? Why? For how long?

3. Are you willing to ask the Holy Spirit to give you the courage and discipline to forgive that person and to even choose to love that person?

4. What is a practical way you can demonstrate love to someone who is difficult for you to like?

Chapter 15
Love First

We love because he first loved us

1 John 4:19

My desire in writing this book has not been to impress anyone with novel and unique concepts but to simply bring into focus what I believe is the cornerstone of our Christian life.

When we grasp the magnitude of God's love for us, we will be inspired to love Him and others above ourselves. He made the first move and that frees us to respond in kind.

> The foundation of Christianity is the Cross of Jesus.

The foundation of Christianity is the Cross of Jesus. Paul professed to know nothing, but Jesus crucified. You may have found this book to be elementary. I hope so. At times it is good to discuss deep theological truths and have debates over doctrines, but it is imperative that we continually come back to a place of simplicity.

I was broken.
I was far from God.

God loved me and gave His Son, Jesus, as a sacrifice for my brokenness.
Through faith in Jesus, I am saved from the consequences of my sin.
Because Jesus loves me and gave His life for me, I am inspired to love Him and to love others.

Now, go and love first.

References:

Anonymous. (2007). *The Kneeling Christian.* Bridge-Logos Publishers.

Bonhoeffer, Dietrich. (1995). *The Cost of Discipleship.* Touchstone.

Brooks, Arthur, C. (2020, February 6). *America's Crisis of Contempt: What I said in my address to the National Prayer Breakfast on Thursday.* Washington Post.https://www.washingtonpost.com/opinions/2020/02/07/arthur-brooks-national-prayer-breakfast-speech/?arc404=true

Collins, Jim. (2001). *Good to Great.* HarperCollins Publishers Inc.

Congregation for the Clergy. (2020, July 31). *Origen against Celsus 414.* Biblia Clerus. http://www.clerus.org/bibliaclerusonline/en/gr5.htm

Emmert, Kevin P. (2014, October 28). *New Poll Finds Evangelicals' Favorite Heresies.* Christianity Today. https://www.christianitytoday.com/ct/2014/october-web-only/new-poll-finds-evangelicals-favorite-heresies.html

Stowell, Joseph M. (1996). *Following Christ: Experiencing Life the Way It was Meant to Be.* Zondervan Publishing House.

Made in United States
Orlando, FL
31 January 2024

43006926R00124